Tom Jones

A Comedy

Joan Macalpine

**Based on the novel by
Henry Fielding**

Samuel French – London
New York – Sydney – Toronto – Hollywood

TOM JONES

This play was commissioned by the Council of Repertory Theatres and by the theatres at Leatherhead, Colchester, Bromley and Salisbury. It was first presented at Leatherhead Theatre on 12 October, 1965, with the following cast:

TOM JONES	*Christopher Bidmead*
SQUIRE ALLWORTHY	*Lindsay Campbell*
BRIDGET ALLWORTHY	*Anne Rutter*
THWACKUM	*Leo Leyden*
BLIFIL	*Richard O'Sullivan*
SQUIRE WESTERN	*Frank Shelley*
MOLLY SEAGRIM	*Elizabeth Bell*
SOPHIA WESTERN	*Jennifer Clulow*
GEORGE SEAGRIM	*Dennis Chinnery*
DOCTOR	*Michael Segal*
HONOUR	*Anne Rutter*
SUSAN	*Mary Grimes*
MRS. WATERS	*Sonia Graham*
MRS. FITZPATRICK	*Helen Lindsay*
BETTY	*Karen Coope*
CAPTAIN FITZPATRICK	*Alan Curtis*
LORD FELLAMAR	*Dennis Chinnery*
CONSTABLE	*Michael Segal*
FIRST BYSTANDER	*Russell Denton*
SECOND BYSTANDER	*George Gallaccio*
WOMAN WITH A BASKET	*Elizabeth Bell*
ANDREWS	*Russell Denton*
ALLWORTHY'S SERVANT	*George Gallaccio*
EXECUTIONER	*Andrew Douglas-Jones*
PRIEST	*George Gallaccio*

Directed by FREDERICK FARLEY
Designed by SIDNEY JARVIS
Stage Director WILLIAM SHARKEY

ACT ONE	Somerset
ACT TWO	Interlude at Upton
ACT THREE	London

Running time, excluding intervals: two hours and ten minutes.

This play was subsequently presented, under the title of *Beset By Women*, by Bernard Delfont at the Prince of Wales Theatre, London, on 9 March, 1966, with the following cast:

TOM JONES	*Keith Barron*
SQUIRE ALLWORTHY	*William Roderick*
BRIDGET ALLWORTHY	*Barbara Bolton*
THWACKUM	*David Nettheim*
BLIFIL	*John Quentin*
SQUIRE WESTERN	*Douglas Blackwell*
MOLLY SEAGRIM	*Elizabeth Bell*
SOPHIA WESTERN	*Virginia Stride*
HONOUR	*Sylvia Bidmead*
DOCTOR	*Walter Hall*
SUSAN	*Carmel Cryan*
MRS. WATERS	*Sonia Graham*
MRS. FITZPATRICK	*Helen Lindsay*
BETTY	*Tina Matthews*
CAPTAIN FITZPATRICK	*Peter Whitbread*
LORD FELLAMAR	*Brian Harrison*
CONSTABLE	*Walter Hall*
WOMAN WITH A BASKET	*Barbara Bolton*
ANDREWS	*Simon Taylor*
ALLWORTHY'S SERVANT	*Paul Barnes*
EXECUTIONER	*Arthur Skinner*
PRIEST	*Peter Boyes*
MAIDS AND BYSTANDERS	*Faith Curtis, Frances Jeater, Norma Vogan, Jonnie Christen, Gerald Deacon, Carl Forgione*

Directed by JORDAN LAWRENCE
Designed by SAXON LUCAS
Stage Director DOUGLAS CORNELISSEN

INTRODUCTION

TOM JONES was commissioned by the theatres at Leatherhead, Colchester, Bromley and Salisbury, and by the Council of Repertory Theatres. It was written, therefore, for small stages (the Leatherhead stage is nineteen feet deep with a twenty-foot proscenium opening) and for small budgets. It needs an auditorium small enough for Tom to speak to the audience in a conversational tone without strain. The keynotes of the production should be simplicity and pace.

In Act I and again in Act III a scene in one place should melt into a scene in another without any pause. If the stage is thought of in areas, this works well. Thus, in Act I, the bedroom, landing, stairs, hallway and upstage centre area where the furniture is, make up Allworthy's house. The downstage right area is Molly's and that entrance leads to her cottage. The downstage left entrance is Western's and his area can extend as far as downstage centre. 'Out of doors' spreads over every part of the stage except the Allworthy home. It is helpful if each area can be defined by lighting, but if this is not possible the actors can establish the areas and leave the lighting to establish mood alone—this is a comedy and needs to be brightly lit.

There are places where the dialogue is designed to cover a given amount of action. For example, Susan's speech while Tom is dressing at the end of Act II should last long enough for him to be dressed and ready to go when she stops talking. It is sufficiently loose-knit for Susan to cut it or repeat it to fit the time needed. Other instances of this sort of thing will come to light once work on the play starts.

As it is a comedy it needs to be played fast, but not at a uniformly breakneck speed. There are some scenes—Tom's first seduction by Molly and Allworthy's deathbed for example—which must not be hurried, and each act ends with a slow passage. The variety of pace is as important as the pace itself.

There were a number of extra effects in the West End production which were valuable there but which are not worth straining after if they cannot be achieved easily. For example, the prison truck gives an attractive picture with a light shining through its high, barred windows, but unless your carpenter has plenty of free time it is not worth the effort of building and setting it up—Tom can enter in chains and the Constable bring a stool for Mrs. Waters when he shows her in.

Most producers will have to dispense with the West End hallway because of sightline difficulties. In that case, the visible bedroom can be as little as four feet above stage level. As long as all entrances to the study, inn parlour and London drawing-room are made either from the stairs or from upstage centre, the convention of place will be happily kept.

The play, like the novel, is a bawdy romp (bawdy, not smutty!) but it is helpful to keep in mind that Fielding's novel also had a serious theme: that the straightforward, generous vices are not the worst ones. Far more evil lies in hypocrisy and that insidious perfection of hypocrisy which is self-deceit—Blifil's kindly villainy must be plausible enough to convince not only himself but also Tom and All-worthy. This theme and the solid certainty of the social order, if they are established, will give a firm backing and framework to the romp itself.

JOAN MACALPINE

ACT I* Somerset

The D.L. entrance is used as the Westerns'. The stairs run down from the half-landing towards the floats. On the left of the half-landing is a door. Opposite the head of the stairs is the door to BRIDGET's *bedroom. Right of this is the door into the visible bedroom, which in this act is* ALLWORTHY's. *The head of* ALLWORTHY's *bed is downstage, and beside it is a small table. On the bed lies the baby, heavily bundled up. Downstairs is* ALLWORTHY's *study. There is a settle to the L. in the study, its back against the side of the staircase. Also in the study are a table and* ALLWORTHY's *armchair to its right, facing the settle across the table. A smaller chair is just to the L. of the table, facing downstage. The groundrow shows a countryside scene, with trees, fields and a village church. Between the downstage pillar and the tree flat D.R. some bushes can just be seen. The D.R. entrance is* MOLLY SEAGRIM's *and has a thatched and dirty awning over it.*

When the curtain rises, TOM *is standing downstage right and only the part of the stage where he is standing is lit. He turns to greet the audience.*

TOM Ladies and gentlemen, good evening. It is my story that we are to tell you tonight: the story of a man who was young, foolish, and not so much a sinner as a man much beset by women. Let my follies earn your honest laughter, as you have been young and foolish. And let my sins be forgiven, as I know they will be forgiven by all gentlemen who have ever felt the power of beauty, and by all ladies whose beauty has ever had power. And as I see none here but the gallant, the beautiful, and those who have in their day been gallant or beautiful, so I hope to win your free forgiveness when all is told and the evening ended.
My story then.
There was, in Somerset, an honest, wise and noble

---

*Paragraph 3 on page ii of this Acting Edition regarding photocopying and video-recording should be carefully read.

hearted magistrate, Squire Allworthy, living with his
sister, Bridget Allworthy.

It happened one evening that Squire Allworthy——

(SQUIRE ALLWORTHY *comes in from U.L. through the
hallway, followed by his manservant, who is carrying
a candle. The lights come up on the study area. The
manservant puts the candle on the table and goes out
the way he came.*)

came home after being away on business for three long
months. He was greeted——

(BRIDGET ALLWORTHY *and* JENNY JONES *appear on the
landing and come downstairs to meet* ALLWORTHY *in the
study.* JENNY *is carrying a candle and the light on the
landing and stairs comes up and fades again as they
come down.*)

by his sister Bridget, still pale after an illness she had
suffered in his absence,

(ALLWORTHY *kisses* BRIDGET.)

and her little maid Jenny Jones——

(JENNY *drops a little curtsy and takes* ALLWORTHY's
cloak and hat.)

ready and to hand to take his cloak and hat. So he was
welcomed home after his long journey, and soon went
upstairs, said goodnight to his sister, and went into his
room.

(JENNY *gives* ALLWORTHY *her candle and takes his cloak
and hat out, through the hallway and off L.* ALLWORTHY
and BRIDGET *go upstairs, part on the landing and go
into their bedrooms,* BRIDGET *into the one at the head
of the stairs and* ALLWORTHY *into the visible one. He
keeps the candle and the lights, which have come with
him up the stairs, now shine on the bedroom.*)

He looked about him—glad to be home after so long—
and then turned to his bed. And there he saw——
me. Me, a baby of a few weeks old. Lying, closely
wrapped up, asleep with my fists by my ears. He flew
to Mistress Bridget's room and called her to see what
he had found. She came, she saw, she was horrified.
But, with a woman's quick wit, she soon guessed what

had happened, and who had committed the crime of being my mother.

(JENNY *returns to the study.* ALLWORTHY *picks up the candle in the bedroom.* BRIDGET *picks up the baby, seizes* ALLWORTHY *by the wrist, and rushes down to confront* JENNY *in the study. The lighting follows the candle downstairs. A tapestry drops in to conceal the visible bedroom.*)

Jenny Jones was charged with having had a baby, in secret. With having concealed the baby from Mistress Bridget, and with having hidden it in Squire Allworthy's bed, hoping that he would adopt it and care for it. Hoping also to avoid being sent to prison for the crime of harlotry. Jenny stood mute at the charge, and did not deny that the child was hers. So Squire Allworthy wondered and grieved and was perplexed, for he thought highly of Jenny, and was unwilling to send her to dark Bridewell prison. At last, seeing his sister taking to the child, he decided to adopt it and bring it up in his own home. He concluded that Jenny was no hardened sinner, and therefore gave her a second chance, finding her a situation away from the village, where she could make a new start and live to repent and be virtuous.

(ALLWORTHY *has seated himself in his chair, R. of the table, and written a brief note. He hands it to* JENNY, *who curtsies and goes out through the hallway and off R.*)

Mistress Bridget, with an eagerness which surprised her brother, took it upon herself to care for the baby.

(BRIDGET *takes one of the candles and goes upstairs, still carrying the baby, and into her bedroom. The lighting follows the candle upstairs.* ALLWORTHY *watches her off.*)

So I was adopted and christened.

ALLWORTHY Tom Jones. (*He sits in his chair, snuffs the candle out and reads.*)

TOM My life began with an act of kindness from Squire

Allworthy, which the world acknowledged by whispering that he must be my real father. Soon afterwards Mistress Bridget married a Captain Blifil, who gave her a son, young master Blifil, and then quickly passed to his heavenly reward, exhausted. A few years later Mrs. Blifil died also, and Squire Allworthy was left with two boys in his charge, and engaged a tutor——

(THWACKUM *enters through the door L. on the landing, reading a book and carrying a cane. He comes downstairs to sit in the study.*)

a Mr. Thwackum, to instruct us. And in time we grew to be young men, Master Jones the bastard and Master Blifil, the Squire's heir, with only eighteen months between us.

(BLIFIL *enters through the door L. on the landing. He comes downstairs and sits, also reading, in the study. The study lighting fades and the out-of-door lighting comes up. During his next sentence* TOM *moves across to downstage D.L.*)

He was studious, but I was forever out of our schoolroom and across the fields, down the stream or in the woods, fishing, riding and shooting. I was forever in trouble for this, too, and never more so than one time when I went shooting with our gamekeeper, Black George Seagrim. And we shot a bird, not over our land, but over our neighbour's.

(*There is a roar offstage L.*)

WESTERN (*off*) Poachers!

TOM   Squire Western. His land : his partridge.

WESTERN (*off*) Poachers. I see un.

TOM   And he saw us. At least he saw me. And gave chase.

(WESTERN *enters D.L. and chases* TOM, *catching him D.R.*)

WESTERN Young varmint. I seed un. Where ha't put un? Thou's hidden un. Where hast got un? (*He searches* TOM *and finds nothing.*) Nay then, t'other took un. I seed un. There were two on ee. Who were he then? Who were with ee?

TOM   Nobody sir. I was alone.

WESTERN Art calling me blind? I seed un. (*He smacks* TOM's *head.*)
Now, thou tell me. Who were un? Who?

TOM There was no one there. I was alone.

WESTERN Drunk, am I? Blind, am I? Deaf and dumb, am I? Para-
lysed up-and-topsidies? I'll give ee alone, alone I'll give
ee. (*He shakes and knocks* TOM *about, and then pushes
him by the scruff of his neck towards the study.*)
There's them as should govern ee. Squire Allworthy
then.
(*The study lights come up and the out-of-door lights
fade.*)

ALLWORTHY Mr Western!

WESTERN Ar, and good day to ee. Drunk and blind, am I? Here's
your young Tom as should be governed by ee. Well
then. Ee be doing something with un.

ALLWORTHY What's Tom been doing?

WESTERN Poaching, that's what. Poaching, and I'd have leathered
him and that been an end to it, but there was another.
Another there was, and he won't be saying.

ALLWORTHY Another?

WESTERN Ah. I've hunted with this boy, and fished with him.
Chased rats round t'barn with him. I seen him grow up
and when I seen him done wrong I leathered him and
no complaints. But when it's poaching, and when there's
another with him and he won't tell me who the other one
were, then I got to make complaints. I'll be to be losing
all my partridge else.

THWACKUM Shot one of your partridge? With an accomplice?

WESTERN Ah. And swears blind he were alone. (*He turns to
BLIFIL.*) Were it you, then? You're of an age, young
Blifil. Were you with un?

BLIFIL No.

THWACKUM Young Mr Blifil was with me and the *Trojan Women*
all evening, sir.

WESTERN Lecherous young devil. Ah, but them white hands never
went poaching. So then. Who were it? Who went with
ee?

TOM No one.

THWACKUM Allow me, Mr Western. If you will leave this young gentleman to me, I flatter myself we shall soon have a confession. (*He flourishes his cane.*)

TOM That you'll not.

WESTERN Ar, you tan it out of un. A hiding, that's what he's lacking. You be a good teacher, Thwackum, you skin his bottom.

TOM You'll not make me tell.

ALLWORTHY Put that cane away, Thwackum. And you stand off him, Mr Western, if you don't mind. Tom, come here. Now Tom, did you go out meaning to poach?

TOM No, sir.

ALLWORTHY Then how did it happen?

TOM There was this partridge, sir. We were near Folly Brook, where your estate meets Squire Western's, and it flew up. I was all excited, sir, and I shot before I thought. It was over Squire Western's land.

ALLWORTHY So it was poaching.

WESTERN I say it and—

ALLWORTHY Western. So it was poaching.

TOM Yes, sir.

ALLWORTHY But then, Tom, if the fellow who was with you goes unpunished, he'll not learn to keep away from poaching. How is Squire Western, how am I, how is any landowner round here, to be easy in our beds, when we don't know who was with you? And how is he to know better? Now Tom, you've to tell me who that was. Tom.

TOM Sir, I—I do wish I could, sir. I do find it hard to refuse you, sir, but—I can't tell anybody, sir.

BLIFIL Tom! Sir, forgive me, but I can't be quiet with him so hard-hearted. Tom, we both owe Mr Allworthy duty, obedience and love. My heart breaks to hear you refuse an answer which all three should make you give. Sir, I cannot share his sin by not telling you.

TOM No!

BLIFIL It was Black George Seagrim with him, sir.

ALLWORTHY George Seagrim?

BLIFIL Yes.

WESTERN Your gamekeeper poaching my game!

ALLWORTHY Not my gamekeeper long at this. Tom, was it George?

TOM I took him. It was my fault, sir.

ALLWORTHY Mr Western, you can be satisfied. There can be no
excuse—a grown man with a good job, and trusted. He
shall be gone from my service tonight.

WESTERN Gamekeeper gone poacher. Ah, and who got better
chances? Who knows better how the game sets? Who's
to slip away easier? Ah, Mr Allworthy, your word and
I'm satisfied. Now you, Tom. No hard feelings: you ride
over to hunting, and my Sophy'll give you your stirrup
cup, friends same as forever. Aye, boy, I leathered ee.
But if ever I catch ee poaching again, I'll none be
leathering ee. I'll be for taking your head and screwing
it right off.

ALLWORTHY I'll be seeing you out, Western. There's an earth through
my upper wood you might like to look at some day.
Young vixen, I think—

(ALLWORTHY *and* WESTERN *go out through the hallway
and off* L.)

TOM (*to* BLIFIL) You know what you've done?

BLIFIL My duty, Tom, and I'm sorry you don't know yours.
Mr Thwackum, there's a part of *Antigone* I'd like you
to look at with me.

THWACKUM Delighted, my boy. Tom!

(TOM *has come downstage away from them.*)

Tom! Ah well. The hand of correction can wait.
Time can but strengthen the strong right arm of affection.

(THWACKUM *and* BLIFIL *go out through the hallway and
off* L. TOM *moves* D.C. *and the study light fades behind
him.*)

TOM I crept away, down to the stream again, horrified by
what I had done. (*He sits.*) My pleasure had taken
George Seagrim shooting and now my pleasure had cost
him his job. He was out of work, and all his children
destitute. Many mouths to be starving at my fault. And
what was to be done? I thought to give him money, but
I had none. All I had of my own were my clothes,
some books and my horse. So my horse became sacrifice

for my conscience: I sold it and took the money to
Black George's cottage.

(*He gets up. Evening lighting comes up on* MOLLY's *area
of the stage*, D.R.)

It was evening when I got there, and his eldest daughter was standing at the door, all alone.

(MOLLY SEAGRIM *enters D.R. and stands twisting her hair
up into a knot. She is a sultry and very dirty slut of
about eighteen.* TOM *goes over to her.*)

MOLLY Evening, sir.

TOM Evening, Molly. Your father in?

MOLLY No, sir. Be gone over to village.

TOM Oh. Thank you.

MOLLY Stop a while and rest. Maybe he'll be back, soon along.

TOM Ah. Good.

MOLLY Sides, the rest is out and all. Be company for me, a little.

TOM Yes.

MOLLY I've not seen much of you. Mr Tom, not these past
weeks. I ain't done nothing, have I, for you to be keeping away?

TOM No, Molly, no.

MOLLY You be growed since I seen you close to. Have I growed
and all?

TOM You've changed.

MOLLY I don't think I've growed. I'm grown woman by now.
Come just over your shoulder, I think I did. Let's be
trying, see where it is now.

TOM Well, I don't—

MOLLY Stand then, and let me try.
(*They stand back to back.*)
There now. You stand still, let me put my hand on my
head. There. Well then, and you have growed. Look.
Good inch that be.

TOM We never measured before.

MOLLY I measured you with my eye, Mr Tom, every time you
come to see father. Watched you grow. You'm a proper
man now. Growed and strong to be looking at. There.
Sit you down then.
(*She pushes him down and sits beside him.*)

I let my hair go, with measuring and all. You'll excuse
if I do it up again?

TOM Of course.

MOLLY I don't know how, it's always coming down, what with
bending to work and—other things. Dark, innit? My
mam said it was along of a ship getting wrecked all
those years back with the Armada. All them Spanish
gentry were dark, she said.

TOM It's pretty.

MOLLY Girls in the village reckon fair's to be beautiful. But I
don't know. I'm happy to be black. Like them as calls
themselves fair is mostly mouse or streaky. There. Is
it up all right now?

TOM Yes, it's all right.

MOLLY It do come down so easy. One touch—if you were to
touch it now, it'd be down, right tumbling down again.
Oh look, there's a bit loose now. It's soft, you feel it
then.
Long time ago, that were, but like my mam said, blood
of the gentry always shows. Comes out, each family.
That's what gives me my feeling for gentry. There now,
Mr Tom, you'll have it all down again, and me only
just putting it up. You're fair, though, alongside of
me. Mr Tom, what you doing? Hold still, you'll tear
it.
(*He kisses her, tearing her blouse.*)
Oh Mr Tom! Why, you ain't never kissed a girl before.

TOM How d'you know?

MOLLY I just guessed. I ain't never been kissed before either.
You didn't ought to have done that. Not out here.

TOM Your father coming home?

MOLLY Oh no. No, not for hours. Might someone come by,
though. Oh look, you did tear it.

TOM Where?

MOLLY By rights you did oughter pin it up again for me.

TOM I haven't got a pin.
(MOLLY *gets up and goes to the* D.R. *exit.*)

MOLLY I got a pin.

TOM Where?

MOLLY My pin's in the cottage. You come and get it?
       (TOM *gets up, eagerly.*)
 TOM I'll come and get it.
MOLLY Dark in there it is. Ain't hardly light enough for
       pinning.
 TOM I'll manage.
MOLLY Reckon you will.
       (*They go out quickly* D.R. TOM *returns immediately*.)
 TOM We found the pin. It was a long hunt, but interesting.
       The first time·in my life I'd had a search like that.
       Molly seemed to be all that was sweet and young and
       innocent.
       (MOLLY *comes in* D.R. *carrying a pin.*)
MOLLY Tom. You never did do me up.
       (TOM *goes to do so.*)
       Do ee love me?
 TOM I love you.
MOLLY No, but for real? Tell me for real.
 TOM For real and for ever.
MOLLY Even after you got what you wanted?
 TOM Even more.
MOLLY I was a good girl. I never done that before. I never been
       kissed before. Kiss me again.
       (*He does.*)
 TOM You know why I kept away, these last weeks? I was
       looking at you, and saying, 'No, I mustn't.'
MOLLY You noticed me?
 TOM Yes.
MOLLY Thought I was pretty?
 TOM Beautiful.
MOLLY But I know what you'll do. I know about men. I heard
       about them. I'm only a village girl. You'll not keep by
       me. You'll pleasure yourself with me, and then you'll
       go off after a gentry girl.
 TOM I won't.
MOLLY All you gentry's the same. I heard you're the same.
       You tell me you love me, till you get what you want.
       You'll be to ruin me and be off.
 TOM I won't just pleasure myself, Molly. I've never been

after a girl before and I love you for ever and all my days.

MOLLY Promise?

TOM Swear it.

MOLLY You do see others. Ladies.

TOM Who then?

MOLLY That Sophia Western. You see her a lot.

TOM I see her father. I go hunting with him.

MOLLY You gave her a linnet.

TOM I gave you more than a linnet. Gave you everything.

MOLLY Oh Tom!

TOM But she might be of use, might Sophia. Useful to you.

MOLLY How?

TOM I'll ask her to help you and your family.

MOLLY She'd never.

TOM If she knew you were starving, she might take you as her maid.

MOLLY You think she would?

TOM I'm sure she would.

MOLLY I do wash a different colour. Oh Tom, would you ask her?

TOM Yes, of course.

MOLLY Then go now and do it. Off Tom, now.

(TOM *goes off* U.R. *and* MOLLY D.R. *As they go the out-of-doors lighting comes up and* SOPHIA *and* BLIFIL *come on* D.L. SOPHIA *is carrying a wicker cage with a bird on a perch inside. There is the sound of a linnet singing.*)

SOPHIA Isn't he pretty, Mr Blifil? And sings so sweetly too.

BLIFIL A wonderful thing, Miss Western, that a little brown bird should have a beautiful voice. Given by God to praise its maker. May I see?

(*He takes the cage. The singing stops.* TOM *reappears* U.R., *but* SOPHIA *and* BLIFIL *do not notice him until he speaks.*)

Yes. Silent now, but a pretty singer, no doubt. You bought it at the market?

SOPHIA No, Mr Blifil, Mr Jones gave him to me.

BLIFIL Mr Jones? But how cruel, Miss Western, to keep it confined in a cage. See how the pretty thing longs for liberty.

(He turns upstage, opens the cage door and puts his hand in, taking the bird off the perch and dropping it on the bottom of the cage where it cannot be seen. Meanwhile he and SOPHIA *seem to watch it fly out of the cage and settle high up on the upstage post.)*

SOPHIA No! Oh no, he's gone! Mr Blifil, he was born in a cage. He'll die in the trees!

TOM I'll get it back.

SOPHIA Oh Mr Jones! It's right up there.

BLIFIL Better die free than live captive.

TOM And I'll deal with you when I've caught it.

BLIFIL I'm not waiting while you play climbing games. I promised to join Mr Thwackum five minutes ago. You'll excuse me, Miss Western?

SOPHIA Do be careful, Mr Jones.

*(*BLIFIL *puts the cage down just out of sight U.R. and goes off U.L.* TOM *has started to climb the upstage post.)*
Oh do be careful!

TOM If I can get near him now, before he's used to being free—

SOPHIA But do be careful. If you fall— Oh!
*(*TOM *slips and falls.)*
No! Please God. Are you hurt? Oh dear. Nothing broken, dear God. Nothing broken? Did that hurt?

TOM No, it tickled.

SOPHIA You shouldn't have gone up there. You might have been killed.

TOM Did the linnet fly?

SOPHIA Yes. Never mind. Don't move just yet. You look pale still and tired. As if you had not slept last night. Have you been over-exerting yourself?

TOM No. No, I— Well, in fact—

SOPHIA Yes?

TOM I have been worried, Miss Western. *(He makes as if to get up.* SOPHIA *pulls him back.)*

SOPHIA Don't move yet. What worried you?

TOM It's George Seagrim, Miss Western. You heard how he lost his job.

SOPHIA Yes.

TOM And it was all my fault. Now he is destitute and his family starving, and I can think of nothing to help them.

SOPHIA Is his family large?

TOM Yes. There is one of them old enough for work, but she has no place as yet. She's right for lady's maid or some such work. Only who will take her now? And those poor children starving. Miss Western, I shall go distracted. What can I do for them?

(SOPHIA *gets up*.)

SOPHIA I think—I think, Mr. Jones, I might help.

(TOM *gets up*.)

TOM Help?

SOPHIA I am myself needing a maid.

TOM There's providence! Oh, but why should you be troubling yourself with my worries.

SOPHIA But if she's young and honest and clean—

TOM She's young and— Well, I found her most teachable.

SOPHIA Then I'll take her. What is her name?

TOM 'Tis Molly. Oh Miss Sophia! Such a kindly thought of yours!

SOPHIA Mr Jones—

TOM Yes?

SOPHIA I do this for pity of their distress, but also for a favour to you, a little. Will you in your turn favour me?

TOM What can I do?

SOPHIA When he goes hunting you go with him, my father.

TOM Yes?

SOPHIA You are young, Mr Jones, and—

TOM Yes?

SOPHIA Only that—that my father— He will not think but that he is young still, and wherever you go, he is bound to follow. You take risks, Mr Jones, you lead him into them also.

TOM You want me to be more careful?

SOPHIA For his sake, Mr Jones. I am always frightened when you go hunting. For him.

TOM And I will be more careful. For you.

SOPHIA Oh. Thank you. My poor linnet is quite flown away.

TOM I will get you another.

SOPHIA I—I should be home by now.

TOM I'll take you back.

SOPHIA I can send for Molly, and see her directly. I hope I shall find her as teachable as you did!

(*They go off D.L. As they go,* MOLLY *runs on U.R. She is wearing a cast-off dress of* SOPHIA's *and is wildly excited. She is pregnant and beginning to show it.*)

MOLLY Honour! Honour! You come out here.

(HONOUR *enters D.R. She is a less extreme version of* MOLLY—*not quite so dirty or so sultry.*)

Look at me then! Look at my dress! That bean't wool, there, that be silk and satin. I be dressed to look a lady. Look there now.

HONOUR What clothes line you get that off? You can't wear that. Everyone'll know you stole it.

MOLLY Did not then.

HONOUR You never got that give you.

MOLLY Did too. Miss Western give it me.

HONOUR What for?

MOLLY Her done send for me. I'm to be her maid. Lady's maid I'm to be.

HONOUR Her gone mad?

MOLLY My Tom asked her. Her's soft for him, and he asked her. He don't make no mind of her, but she'd walk the world barefoot for him. Only he ain't for her.

HONOUR Aye, but he's been for you then, and it's coming to show and all.

MOLLY I ain't got nothing showing!

HONOUR 'Satin above and silk below
    Whatever the clothes the sin will show.'

MOLLY You're jealous.

HONOUR I'm none jealous. I got my virtue.

MOLLY Only for want of a buyer. Lady's maid. Her told me to wash.

HONOUR There's no washing going to wash away what's coming for you.

MOLLY Perhaps I'll tell Miss Western I got a sister needs a job. Maybe scrubbing floors. If you wash. (*She goes out D.R.*)

HONOUR   Wash, she said. Now wouldn't Miss Western prefer the virtuous sister if she were clean and all? Ar. Her'll not last a month. I'll get our Dad to give me a good scrub down.

(HONOUR *goes out* D.R. *As she goes,* TOM *comes in* D.L.)

TOM   Honour was right. Within a fortnight Molly was arrested and taken before Squire Allworthy, Justice of the Peace for the parish. She was accused of harlotry. I heard of it while I was dining with Squire Western and Sophia, and rushed from the table, my haste showing everyone that I had a part in Molly's downfall. I went straight home and there I found Mr Allworthy, with Mr Thwackum as his clerk, sitting in judgement on my Molly.

(*As* TOM *has been speaking,* THWACKUM *has brought* MOLLY *in* U.R., *walked with her across just below the cyclorama, and into the hallway.* ALLWORTHY *comes through the hallway from the* L. *and into the study where he sits in his chair.* THWACKUM *follows him into the study and sits upstage of the table, taking notes of the proceedings.* MOLLY *stands to face* ALLWORTHY. *The out-of-doors lighting fades and the study lighting comes up. As he finishes speaking,* TOM *moves over to stand ready to enter through the hallway into the study from the* R.)

ALLWORTHY   Molly Seagrim, your sin is past denying, and it would be easy enough to send you to Bridewell and let the parish wash its hands of you. You have heard of Bridewell?

MOLLY   Yes, sir.

ALLWORTHY   That it is a terrible place?

MOLLY   Yes.

ALLWORTHY   If you be a harlot, there is no place else for you, soon or late. But if this be a single sin and you repent it, I should be guilty myself to send you among criminals. Now tell me: was this crime or sin?

MOLLY   It weren't no crime, sir.

ALLWORTHY   Then you must tell me the name of your seducer.

MOLLY What?

ALLWORTHY Your seducer.

MOLLY Who's that then?

ALLWORTHY The father. The man.

MOLLY You mean my sweetheart?

ALLWORTHY Yes.

MOLLY But I can't tell.

ALLWORTHY Can't tell?
(TOM *rushes through the hallway and into the study,
where he stands panting and waiting to speak.*)
Tom? What is it?

TOM Sir, I, I've only just heard. You mustn't be sending Molly
to Bridewell.

ALLWORTHY Why? What part have you in this?

TOM It was me, sir. I was to blame, not her.

ALLWORTHY You seduced this girl?

TOM Sir.

THWACKUM Thomas, Thomas!

MOLLY I hadn't told on you, Tom. Don't you be hard on him,
sir. Squire Western says a man's not a man till he's
got his bastard.

THWACKUM Silence better tokens penitence, child. You are sinful,
and likely to be a charge upon the parish.

MOLLY I won't be no charge, sir. Don't ee send me to Bridewell,
sir. I won't be no charge. He never promised marriage, sir.
It were just a bit of fun. Bit of sin. (*Wheedling.*) Sir?

ALLWORTHY Mr Thwackum, take her home, if you please.

MOLLY You won't send me to Bridewell?

ALLWORTHY No. I will see tomorrow what is to be done for you.

MOLLY Thank you, sir. I am grateful, sir. It weren't very sinful,
sir. I mean he didn't quite force me.

THWACKUM Come, child.

MOLLY I know the way.

THWACKUM My guidance shall be spiritual. A man's protecting arm—
Come, child.
(THWACKUM *and* MOLLY *go out through the hallway, and
back the way they came.*)

ALLWORTHY And you know, Tom, the sorrow such a child inherits,
born without a father.

TOM Yes, sir.

ALLWORTHY You found her innocent?

TOM Yes.

ALLWORTHY You made her promises?

TOM No. It was for love, sir.

ALLWORTHY She loves you.

TOM She's a simple, straightforward girl, sir. I seemed to love her too.

ALLWORTHY You seemed?

TOM I thought I would love her forever, sir, but then it seemed to wear away, somehow. I never thought about a child, sir.

ALLWORTHY Never thought?

TOM No. Well—well, at first it just happened, and then afterwards—well, nothing came of it, so I thought nothing ever would.

ALLWORTHY You thought little enough. This is a fault of passion, Tom. That you should take and ruin a village girl, whose family can give no help nor yet protection. And that you, who know what a bastard suffers, should thoughtlessly bring bastardy to birth. What answer, what defence, what excuse can you give for this?
(*He waits for an answer, but* TOM *cannot find anything to say.*)
There is a little in your favour, that I think you acted without premeditated viciousness. And you have confessed your fault to save the girl. She shall be provided for. Now think, Tom, of all the evil this intemperance brings. I would have you a man, Tom, to rule your passions with reason. Let you cease to be an ungoverning child. You are a man in growth and power of evil: would I could see such manhood in control and a power for good.
(ALLWORTHY *goes out through the hallway and off* L. TOM *comes ruefully down to speak to the audience. The study lights fade behind him.*)

TOM If we'd been Papists then, I'd have joined a monastery. But then I thought of Sophia. You've seen Sophia. Could any man be a man and not love her? And there I was, bound in honour to foolish, mucky Molly. You husbands will tell me that being bound to one woman is sure to make you fancy another. But you have seen them both and you can see that Molly is for—tickling, and Sophia for sticking with. Yet Molly loved me. Molly had given me her innocence and her trust—and a son for good measure. I could never abandon her or hurt her, but I did begin to wonder whether her love might not be pressed to death under a sufficient weight of metal. (*He chinks the money in his pocket.*) So I went to see her, bursting in with the full confidence of an acknowledged lover.

(*The evening lighting on* MOLLY's *part of the stage comes up.* TOM *hurries over towards the D.R. entrance.*)

Molly!

(MOLLY, *in her nightdress, enters D.R. and intercepts him. She is somewhat agitated but doing her best not to show it.*)

MOLLY   Why, Tom!

TOM   Molly! Aren't you well? What are you doing in bed?

MOLLY   Nothing, dear. You wait till I get dressed?

TOM   What should I wait for? I'll lend you a hand. (*He starts for the door. She stops him.*)

MOLLY   No, Tom. I—I thought Squire Allworthy forbade you to come to see me.

TOM   Yes, he did.

MOLLY   So I never thought you'd come.

TOM   Aren't you glad to see me? Give us a kiss then.

MOLLY   No, Tom, no. Not now. Not just like this, here.

TOM   Come in then, I want to talk to you.

MOLLY   No, Tom. Now we don't want to risk offending Squire Allworthy.

TOM   No, we don't, Molly, that's what I've been thinking about.

MOLLY   You've been thinking about it, but you come here? Without giving me notice?

TOM   That's why I came. To tell you what I thought. Seriously, Molly. One of us must think seriously, and as I am the man—

MOLLY Yes, Tom, but not now—

TOM There comes a time when simple pleasure must end, and I must forget my own happiness and plan for your future life.

(*For the first time* MOLLY *gives* TOM *her full attention.*)

MOLLY My what?

TOM We've got to think of the future.

MOLLY (*wailing*) You're tired of me!

TOM No.

MOLLY You're my gentleman!

TOM Of course I am. Only we can't marry, and no one will take you till we're parted. And you with a little money to your marriage.

MOLLY You're looking to be rid of me!

TOM Your future—

MOLLY That's your love, to ruin a poor girl and forsake her. My mother said never take with a gentleman, they swear and swear till they get their way, and it don't mean two straws in a duckpond. You be a perjury man, like all the gentry.

TOM No, Molly—

MOLLY What do signify all the riches of the world? All the men there be, I never could love another man all the days of my life. Not if the greatest squire of the county came a-suiting me tomorrow, I wouldn't give him my company.

TOM Don't shout out here—

MOLLY What do signify to be silent, when my heart is broke?

TOM Here, come in. (*He tries to pull* MOLLY *through the door. She desperately pulls him back.*)

MOLLY No!

TOM (*looking offstage*) What's that there then?

MOLLY Tain't nothing. Tis my sister.

TOM (*calling*) Come out there.

MOLLY Leave her be, tis Lizzie. You stay where you are.

TOM (*threateningly*) Come or I'll get you! Come now!

(*There is a pause. Then* THWACKUM *sidles on from* MOLLY's *room. He is wearing a nightshirt and his feet are bare.* MOLLY *bursts into tears.*)

MOLLY   What you want to come out for? I told you keep hid
         there. I'm ruined now, ruined for good and forever I
         am.
         (TOM *recovers from his astonishment and roars with
         relieved laughter.*)

TOM   My apologies, oh I do apologise, Mr Thwackum! To
         interrupt you with a new pupil!

THWACKUM You may be pleasant, sir, and you may look forward
         to exposing me—

TOM   Nay sir, I think you've exposed yourself already! Teach-
         ing her to decline and fall, were you?

THWACKUM You may be pleasant, you may be pleasant, sir. But I
         am not the one who corrupted innocence here. I was
         not at fault in that.

TOM   Not you nor half the parish.

MOLLY   Tom!

TOM   Oh my sweet corruption! Dear easy heart. Come now,
         dry your eyes and back to work. There's good honest
         money there, more than ever you'd get from me. Be
         kind to her, my tutor, and I'll never open my lips of
         how your legs are hairy. There, Molly. Be faithful to
         him, and good luck to us all.
         (*He goes D.L. and sits on the stairs, still chuckling, until*
         MOLLY *and* THWACKUM *have gone.*)

MOLLY   Tom! Tom! (*She turns to* THWACKUM.) There now, I
         told you stay still. You lost me the prettiest gentleman,
         and he were my gentleman, and he were for love he
         were, my dear Tom, not an old doctored pussy like you!

THWACKUM Dear girl!

MOLLY   With your pot belly and your hammer toe! Get back
         in the dark there, I can't bear to see you!

THWACKUM Now Molly, love. My dear.

MOLLY   In there then!
         (*She drives him off D.R.* TOM *gets up and comes D.L. as
         the out-of-door lighting comes up.*)

TOM   Free, free, free! And there was Will Barnes, her sister
         said, had her before me. Free forever, to think forever
         of Sophia, sweet, good, tender, unconscious, inaccessible,
         unattainable Sophia.

(SOPHIA *has come on D.L. and* TOM *almost collides with her. He speaks before he can stop himself.*)
Oh Miss Western, I do love you.

SOPHIA Mr Jones!

TOM (*overcome with confusion*) No, I don't. I didn't mean to say that. Miss Western. Please. Could you forget I said—I mean, I mustn't. I can't do that. Not with you. Your father and Mr Allworthy wouldn't either of them, not let us, with me being landless and a—and my birth. There is no way in honour and my thoughts of you are all in honour. So please. Forget what I said.
(SOPHIA *conceals her delight at his declaration.*)

SOPHIA I am sure you cannot have meant what you said, except as a passing fancy. And as you say, it is not possible. So I have. I have forgotten it already, Mr Jones.

TOM Thank you, Miss Western.

SOPHIA I hope we may still be friends. And talk of entirely indifferent topics.

TOM Yes, indeed I hope so.

SOPHIA How wonderfully these fine days are lingering on. One would think autumn would last forever.

TOM It will last forever, you know.

SOPHIA We speak of the weather.

TOM Yes, Miss Western. It is a lovely day. The autumn is beautiful. Sad.

SOPHIA Yet how clear and calm. Look how straight the smoke goes up from George Seagrim's cottage there.

TOM Yes. But in this light isn't it clear what a dark, low hut it is.

SOPHIA And yet, softened by distance, it could be thought attractive.

TOM Not when one has climbed up to stand here with you, and see things clearly.

SOPHIA In this autumn sunshine.

TOM (*looking at her*) All this—distant beauty.

SOPHIA And the trees, I don't think they're ever going to lose their leaves this year, or the birds stop singing. But look there. That bird's all by itself, perched there, and silent.

TOM It's not a linnet.

SOPHIA   My linnet will be dead now.

TOM   If I hadn't slipped—

SOPHIA   I thought you were dead.

TOM   I must not talk about it, but it's not a passing fancy. Look. (*He takes a ring off his finger.*) It's as lasting as this and I never will mention it again. But can I give you this to wear, to remind you silently that since I may not look at you, I can never look at any other woman?

SOPHIA   No, Mr Jones, I mustn't. I mustn't allow—encourage—

TOM   You won't, you don't. I don't want you to love me, that would only make two of us miserable, but please take it, wear it.

SOPHIA   No. No, you must keep it—
(SQUIRE WESTERN *is heard calling, off* L.)

WESTERN   Tom!

SOPHIA   My father. Quick! (*She grabs the ring and puts it on.*)

WESTERN   (*off*) You seen young Mr. Jones? Tom! (*He comes in* D.L.)
There now. You be deaf? I been looking for you all over.

TOM   I'm sorry, sir.

WESTERN   You be getting home now. Quick now. They been to be sending for you and you not been home these three days. There's Allworthy took a fever, lad, and not to last till morning. You'd best get back there.

TOM   Ill? How long?

WESTERN   You be getting home to find out.

TOM   Yes. Now.

WESTERN   Best you had. Come on then, Sophy, and don't you be for to cry. You know I can't abide it.

SOPHIA   (*upset*) Mr. Jones—

TOM   Yes.

WESTERN   There now, lad. Ill news is oft belied by time. Give un our best respects if he'm well enough to bear it.
(TOM *goes* U.C. *and waits to enter the study through the hallway.*)
Come now, Sophy. Ah now, 'tis noted truth: small drinkers die young.

(WESTERN *and* SOPHIA *go out* D.L. *The out-of-doors lighting fades and lights come up on the study and stairs.*
THWACKUM *and* BLIFIL *come down the stairs into the
study, carrying cutlery boxes and an inventory. They
are bustling and very busy.*)

THWACKUM Man that is born of woman hath but a short time to
live, and is full of misery. He cometh up and is cut
down, like a flower. He fleeth as it were a shadow and
never continueth in one stay. Put those down there
and let us check them off in an orderly way. In the
midst of life we are in death: two dozen of teaspoons.
(BLIFIL *sits in* ALLWORTHY's *chair and checks off the
items on the inventory.*)

BLIFIL We brought nothing into this world, and it is certain
we carry nothing out. The Lord gave and the Lord
taketh away. There's a fork missing.

THWACKUM Note it down and see if it's in the kitchen. Behold thou
hast made my days as it were a span long, and mine
age is even as nothing in respect of thee—
(TOM *has come into the study.*)

TOM Mr. Thwackum, is my father dead?

THWACKUM In the midst of life we are in death. The knives are all
here. Ah, Thomas, this day is sorrowful.

TOM Is he dead?

THWACKUM He lingers, my boy, he lingers. But the fever is sore
upon him.

TOM He's still alive?

THWACKUM Teach us to number our days, that we may apply our
hearts unto wisdom.

TOM And you're checking your inheritance?

BLIFIL It would be ungrateful to rebel against the will of God,
Tom. He would wish that all should be in order.

TOM Then take it out of here! He's just upstairs. Take it out!

BLIFIL Hush. Don't let our natural grief make you intemperate.

THWACKUM Patience. Quiet resignation to the will of heaven. We
were about to move on into the kitchen.

TOM Then go.
(THWACKUM *and* BLIFIL *go out, through the hallway
and off* L. TOM *climbs the stairs. As he does so the*

tapestry concealing the bedroom is lifted and the bed-room lighting comes up, revealing ALLWORTHY *restless and moaning in bed.* TOM *enters the bedroom.*)
Not dead. Oh, my father. (*He straightens the bedclothes over him and adjusts the pillows.*) There. There now. That should be better. You're burning. Quiet then, quiet. Rest quiet. Oh my friend, my father. Gently. Gently. Oh Lord, let him not die while he has yet cause to be displeased with me. Father in heaven, give him strength. Strengthen him. Save him. Keep him here.
(*The* DOCTOR *comes in from* L. *through the hallway, followed by* THWACKUM *and* BLIFIL.)

DOCTOR   Worse, you say? I feared it, I feared it.

BLIFIL   To all our griefs. Sinking, I fear.

DOCTOR   Feared it, feared it. Should have been called in sooner. Neglect of a fever at first has caused more deaths than I can count.

BLIFIL   In the midst of life—

DOCTOR   I'll go up then.

BLIFIL   Ease his passing if you can. (*A dreadful thought strikes him.*) Mr. Thwackum, the cutlery!

THWACKUM   In the kitchen—

BLIFIL   Not locked up! Check it all again!
(THWACKUM *and* BLIFIL *hurry out through the hallway and off* L. *The* DOCTOR *goes upstairs and into* ALL-WORTHY'S *bedroom.*)

DOCTOR   Good evening there. Mr. Jones, is it?

TOM   Doctor?

DOCTOR   And how are we, then? Excuse.
(TOM *gets out of the* DOCTOR'S *way, moving to stand by the door. The* DOCTOR *takes* ALLWORTHY'S *pulse, feels his forehead, looks into his eyes, and pulls the covers up over his shoulders.*)
Yes. Yes. Yes, indeed.

TOM   He's dying.

DOCTOR   Absolute quiet, Mr. Jones. Absolute peace and quiet. No disturbance in here at all. Nothing to break his sleep at all.

TOM   Sleep?

DOCTOR A very healthy sign. Fever broken. Sleep. Quiet. Peace. Yes. We have, I think, brought the fever to a perfect remission.

TOM I thought he was dying.

DOCTOR No, no. No, no, no. Sleep was coming. All should be well. Now. Out with you. Take your young noise elsewhere. (*He ushers* TOM *out on the landing.*)

TOM Thank God then.

DOCTOR Indeed yes.
(*He goes back into the bedroom and closes the door as the bedroom lighting fades and the tapestry comes down again.* TOM *comes down to the half-landing, over-joyed at the news.*)

TOM Blifil! Thwackum. Blifil, Blifil, here then!
(BLIFIL *and* THWACKUM *come in, carrying the boxes of cutlery and the inventory.*)

THWACKUM Hush, hush. This is a house of mourning.

TOM It's not, it's not then!

THWACKUM The Lord giveth, the Lord taketh—what's not what?

TOM Not mourning. (*He comes down the remaining stairs and the staircase lighting fades.*) Oh my brother, he's better. He's sleeping.

BLIFIL Not dying?

TOM No. He'll be well again. No need to count these.
(*He crosses below* BLIFIL, *hitting the cutlery boxes as he passes him, and moves D.R.*)

BLIFIL Is this certain?

THWACKUM Nothing is certain on this earth, my boy. The Lord taketh, the Lord giveth back again. Strength yet, however. There may yet be a relapse!
(*They carry the boxes and inventory out through the hallway and off L. The study lighting fades as they go, and the out-of-doors lighting comes up.*)

TOM No relapse. He's well, he's sleeping. And if he's well, there's nothing wrong. I can live to please him. I can rise above all the weakness and sinfulness I've ever known. I can look at Sophia from a distance and be content with no more. Pure and purged and uplifted forever. Never to sin, never to be weak again.

(MOLLY *pops out near him. She is no longer pregnant.*)

MOLLY Evening, master Tom.

TOM What? Molly!

MOLLY Lovely evening, master Tom.

TOM Wonderful. Oh Molly, it is! Mr. Allworthy's well!

MOLLY Took bad, was he?

TOM We thought he was dying.

MOLLY Ah. The poor gentleman. Gave me money, he did, and boarded the baby and never asked for anything—you know—in return.

TOM He's all goodness. Molly, whose was the baby?

MOLLY Mine, of course.

TOM But who was its father?

MOLLY Bless you, Mr. Tom, I don't know.

TOM And I thought you were sweet.

MOLLY Well, aren't I?

TOM Young and innocent.

MOLLY Who wants that? I were fun. Weren't I fun now?

TOM Yes, you were fun.

MOLLY And it's months since I seen you to talk to. There now. Give us a kiss for old time's sake.

TOM It's all over, you know.

MOLLY Arr.
(*They kiss.*)

TOM Finished and forgotten.

MOLLY Arr.
(*They kiss.*)

TOM Repented and forgiven.

MOLLY Arr.
(*They dive off behind the bushes* U.R. THWACKUM *and* (BLIFIL *come on through the hallway from* L. *and come a little downstage between the posts.* THWACKUM *has a walking stick.*)

THWACKUM Drunk, I tell you.

BLIFIL Surely not.

THWACKUM Drunk and shouting and—in a house of sickness.

BLIFIL We must be sorry, not angry.
(*He has wandered* U.R. *and glances behind the bushes.*)
Oh no! Gracious heavens! How terrible.

THWACKUM What is it, boy? What's the matter?

BLIFIL In those bushes. Oh dear. There is some wicked purpose there.

THWACKUM What did you see?

BILFIL Nothing. No, no. It may not have been Tom.

THWACKUM Thomas? In the bushes?

(*He goes to look.* BLIFIL *restrains him, half-heartedly.*)

BLIFIL No, no. I cannot be sure. And I couldn't see at all who the wench was.

THWACKUM With a wench? A slut?

BLIFIL No, Mr. Thwackum, I don't know. It was a fellow and a female, but I cannot swear it was Tom, and their purpose may surely yet have been innocent.

THWACKUM Innocent! Nothing innocent can happen in a bush! This is what comes of kindness to bastards. I blame Mr. Allworthy, I fear I do. His leniency has encouraged vice on every hand. Hush.

(*They stand listening.* MOLLY *giggles and squeaks offstage.*)

As his patron lies sick, he's at it again. Turn away, master Blifil, while I expose this iniquity.

(*He advances on the noise.* TOM *emerges and bars his way.*)

Well, I knew it was you! Is there a maiden in the village you have not debauched? Out of my way, sir. I must know who shares your sin.

TOM Why? Do you want to be next?

(THWACKUM *strikes at* TOM *with his stick.* TOM *seizes the end of it and they tug for possession.*)

BLIFIL Tom. Tom. Lawful authority, Tom!

(BLIFIL *joins in to get the stick from* TOM. TOM *lets it go so that* THWACKUM *sits down suddenly, while* TOM *knocks* BLIFIL *down.* THWACKUM *gets up and moves towards the bushes.* TOM *seizes his coat-tails and pulls him back. They fight and* TOM *knocks* THWACKUM *down and holds him down.* BLIFIL, *recovering, pulls* TOM *off* THWACKUM, *and* BLIFIL *and* THWACKUM *both set on* TOM. *He is getting the worst of it when* SQUIRE WESTERN

comes in with SOPHIA *on his arm, coming from* D.L.
WESTERN *has a walking stick.*)

WESTERN By, Sophy, look, a fight.

SOPHIA Father, look—

WESTERN They'm going it. Nay then, two on to one's not fair.
Hey then, hold up, I'm here, I'm with ee.
(*He plunges into the mêlée. For a moment he and*
THWACKUM *parry the blows of each other's sticks, while*
TOM *defeats* BLIFIL.)
Out, out for shame, the pair on you. Can you not fight
fair? There. There.

THWACKUM Nay, sir, nay. No wish to fight. No, no. My cloth, sir,
remember my cloth. Pray desist. Ow!

WESTERN And be still then. I'll have none but fair fights about me.

SOPHIA Oh, he's bleeding! Oh my dear!
(*She reaches in the general direction of* TOM *and* BLIFIL,
each of whom has blood on his face, and faints.)

TOM Sophia!
(*He runs to pick her up.* WESTERN *goes to her as well.*)

WESTERN Nay, the gurt boobies, for shame, what you've done.
Nay, give her to me lad, th'art all bloody. Stand off,
give her air. There, my pretty, there. What for you be
fighting, tutor, man of your age?

THWACKUM The cause is near enough. Beat the bushes well, you
may find her.

WESTERN You been fighting for a wench?

THWACKUM Ask that gentleman there. He best knows who it was.

WESTERN Nay then, it were a wench and all.

THWACKUM By now the harlot is gone.

WESTERN Gurt spoilsport. Nay Tom, still at it, art a? Th'art me
at thy age, lad.

THWACKUM I have to say it: you encourage vice, Mr. Western.

WESTERN Nay, there's some as can and there's others is jealous.
Aye, and look what hast done to my Sophy. Get ee off
and wash they faces. Nay, my pretty. Get ee off then,
all on yer.

TOM Can I help you with—

WESTERN Nay nay, let her lie quiet. She'll do. Women's forever
fainting, don't ee make no mind.

TOM I'll be over tomorrow.

WESTERN Aye then.
(TOM *follows* THWACKUM *and* BLIFIL *off, going* U.C. *through the hallway and off* L. SOPHIA *begins to revive.*)
There now, there now, my pretty. Gently, now gently. Don't ee come up sudden. Rest a minute now.

SOPHIA Where is he—they— What happened, Father?

WESTERN Why, they had done with fighting and are off to wash they bloody faces.

SOPHIA Was—were any of them hurt?

WESTERN Now puss, don't ee be tricksy with me. I know the way the wind lies.

SOPHIA Father?

WESTERN Do ee think I'm blind then? Your old father, eh? Who was bleeding then? And who was crying out to see un hurt, and fainting clean away? And if I said one of them was near to be killed?

SOPHIA Which one?

WESTERN Aye, that's changed thy colour. Ee thought I'd be angry, aye and I tell ee, a father's a right to be angry if his daughter goes falling in love without asking his leave.

SOPHIA No, father—

WESTERN Ah, but I bain't angry. Never was angry with ee, Sophy, nor ever will be, long as ee don't cross my wishes. Aye. Tell ee, lass. Hast chosen where I'd have set my mind. Never thought of my girl getting married, but if her wants that one, her shall have him. Tell ee. I'll be round to see old Allworthy to be settling the matter with him.

SOPHIA You like him, father? You'd let me marry him?

WESTERN That I would. Fact, now I've got idea into my head, 'tis a good idea and I'll *make* ee marry un. Hey then. Art pleased, lass?

SOPHIA Oh father! (*She kisses him.*)

WESTERN There, lass, there. None the old bear, am I? Sweet and gentle as a lamb I be, long as I gets my way. Now. Can'st walk, lass? Nay, I've put roses in thy cheeks.

SOPHIA I never dared to hope you'd let me marry him. (*She kisses him again.*)

WESTERN He shall marry thee. Aye, and if he won't I'll leather
him into it. Aye then.
(*He beckons to* HONOUR, *who comes in from D.L. carrying a chair. She sets it D.C., and goes out D.L. The upstage lighting fades, leaving only the downstage area
L. and C. brightly lit.*)
Ee be sitting there, and I'll send him to ee, soon as he
gets here. And no forwardness. Let him ask afore ee
says yes. (*He goes out D.L. and is heard speaking, off.*)
Aye lad, int best clothes?

SOPHIA He's here. How shall I support myself? No. It's but to
say what he's said already. I know his heart, and he
knows mine. Nothing can go wrong. It's just a moment's
awkwardness.

WESTERN (*off*) In there, lad. And don't ee be shy. If her's okkard,
kiss her.

SOPHIA Oh!
(*She sits down, her back half-turned to the D.L. entrance, through which* BLIFIL *enters. He stands for a
moment, but she does not look up. He clears his throat
but she still does not look at him. After another pause
he clears his throat again and speaks.*)

BLIFIL Miss Western.

SOPHIA Oh!
(*She jumps as if she had been shot. Her jumping makes*
BLIFIL *jump too.*)

BLIFIL Miss Western!

SOPHIA (*backing away*) No. No, Mr. Blifil, no!

BLIFIL You cannot say no, Miss Western. I haven't asked you
yet.

SOPHIA I beg your pardon. (*She sits down again.*)

BLIFIL Miss Western, we both know what I have come for,
and I do want to spare you awkwardness or embarrass-
ment, so I will be entirely open with you.

SOPHIA No, but—

BLIFIL Don't disquiet yourself for a moment: I wish to put
you at your ease.

SOPHIA Mr. Blifil—

BLIFIL Just let me speak—

SOPHIA Please—

BLIFIL —if possible without interruption. Your worthy father tells me that you have conceived a violent passion for me and that that was why you fainted. Now I know that many men would feel that to fall in love without your father's having suggested it is immodest and forward. But I assure you that I don't believe you are habitually forward or immodest. So please: don't disquiet yourself. I can overlook the slight indecorum.

SOPHIA (*desperate*) Please, Mr. Blifil.

BLIFIL No, don't thank me! To put you entirely at ease I will add that the possibility of such an alliance had occurred to me also. In fact the advantages of the match are overwhelming. You must have felt excitement at the possibilities. Your father's land and Mr. Allworthy's march side by side: combined they will make the largest estate in Somerset. (*He is getting carried away by these glowing prospects.*) Have you thought about the possibility of breeding?

SOPHIA No.

BLIFIL You should, you should. The combined estates and the combined herds will make selective breeding for milk or beef a real possibility. Dear Miss Western, I would marry you for your grazing alone!

SOPHIA Oh. Thank you.

BLIFIL It had not occurred to you?

SOPHIA No, I must confess.

BLIFIL Strange. Now there indeed would have been an excuse for impetuosity. But I meant *not* to remind you of that. Though I was surprised to find that there was no feeling about my foster-brother to come between us.

SOPHIA Mr. Jones? Why, what should I feel about him?

BLIFIL Fear, Miss Western. Fear that my uncle's partiality for Tom might end in Tom's inheriting too large a portion of the estate. But I think I can reassure you there. As time passes and Tom's indiscretions are judiciously brought to notice, I think we can be sure that Tom's share of the inheritance will shrink to very reasonable proportions, even if he is not disinherited altogether.

SOPHIA   Oh.

BLIFIL   You were not to know this, of course, which still shows impetuosity. However, marriage to me will cure the rash passion of your nature, and I know that you will make me a frugal, sober and industrious housekeeper.

SOPHIA   Thank you.

BLIFIL   And as such a fit mother for my offspring. Such as it may please God. I think we can congratulate ourselves. It is fitting that two such noble estates should come together for the procreation of children to be brought up in the fear and nurture of the Lord. Not, as he says, to satisfy carnal lusts and appetites. But as a remedy against sin. For you. Yes, I think we may sleep—no, no—rest easy in the knowledge that in this alliance we do our duty to our families, our inheritance and certainly, as an example, to the poor of both parishes.

SOPHIA   No, Mr. Blifil, I beg of you. I must tell you—

BLIFIL   No, no. We must beware of any further immodesty on your part. You have given me all the encouragement propriety allows.
(WESTERN *looks in* D.L.)

WESTERN   Ho-ho? Kissing yet? Cuddling? Hast made her blush, young man? Fore George, I've always thought ee a cold fish, but I reckon you'll tumble her yet.

BLIFIL   Your daughter has answered the warmth of my suit with every encouragement modesty will permit. If I may, I will take leave now, and entrust the formal arrangements to my uncle and yourself. Goodbye, sir. Goodbye, Miss Western.
(SOPHIA *cannot speak.*)

WESTERN   Goodbye, lad.
(BLIFIL *goes* D.L.)

SOPHIA   Father!

WESTERN   There, lass, art happy now?

SOPHIA   Father! (*She bursts into tears.*)

WESTERN   Nay then, Sophy, hast pleased thy old father. Aye then, haven't I said ee were't prettiest maid i' Somerset? And best and sweetest, and ee'll none be less pretty for being married. Hey then. Make the first a boy, what dost say? Ee'd do that for't old father? Ah Sophy, Sophy, art they father's treasure, and I do be foolish fond on ee.

SOPHIA You do want for me to be happy?

WESTERN That I do, my pretty. More than anything.

SOPHIA Then please sir, I do beg of you: let nothing more be said of Mr. Blifil.

WESTERN What?

SOPHIA I want to stay at home with you, father. I don't want to leave you.

WESTERN Who's leaving me? Ull be in't next parish.

SOPHIA But I can't be happy with him.

WESTERN (*with determination*) We'm talking marriage, not happiness.

SOPHIA You can't want to make me miserable. I shall die of the horror of it if I have to marry him.

WESTERN Die? Stuff. None died of marriage yet.

SOPHIA I'm not even indifferent to him. I hate him! I detest the sight of him!

WESTERN Hate? Detest?

SOPHIA Yes.

WESTERN Hate and detest as much as ee likes. Ee'll have un. I fixed it: I've arranged it, and I've set my heart on it. My girl, you try me out of all patience.
(TOM *comes in D.L.*)

TOM Sir? Oh. (*Seeing a scene is in progress, he turns to go.*)

WESTERN Nay then, come here, lad. Th'art a man, and a friend, and I be sore vexed.

TOM Is Miss Western ill?

WESTERN She'm right as a trivet. Tell ee, Tom, her fancied young Blifil, and I get her young Blifil, and damn me if her ain't taken agin him and asking leave and talking detesting.
(SOPHIA *looks beseechingly at* TOM.)

TOM She doesn't like him?

WESTERN What counts if she do or she don't? Her father likes his land. This be nowt but the way of all maids. Her mother were just the same, afore she married me. Vapouring and fainting and threatening to die. And what came of it? I tell ee, my young lady, her pa took a stick to her, and her was glad to marry me, for all at wedding breakfast her couldn't sit down. Aye, and lucky she were to get me, and a happy woman, till she took it into her head to die of a decline. Now then. I tell ee, young lady. I ha' set my heart on young Blifil, and art marrying him, or begging bread in rags.

TOM Sir—please—I've known Miss Western so long. Might I perhaps—do you think I could try—could have a word in private with her?

WESTERN Don't ee try reasoning. They'm none reasonable creatures.

TOM Let me try. Let me try talking to her.

WESTERN Art my friend, Tom. Aye. Tell her. Try what can'st do. She'll break my heart, and I'll break her neck, if she do rest stubborn.

TOM Thank you, sir. Right alone, then.

WESTERN Aye aye. Alone.

(WESTERN *goes out* D.L. TOM *leads* SOPHIA, *still weeping, to the chair.*)

TOM No, dear. Gently. Gently. Sit down. There now. Hush, my dearest, quietly now. He can't force you. No power on earth can force you. And he loves you. He may bluster and shout for a while, but he'll not turn you out.

SOPHIA Mr. Jones, I wish I were dead!

TOM And what would I do then?

SOPHIA All I am now is a cause of vexation to my father, and suffering to you.

TOM All you are is love. Now stay on earth for my sake. Only promise me never, never, never to let them force you into marrying Blifil.

SOPHIA I never could. I'd sooner marry a toad.

TOM And good reason. I've heard of many a toad turned into a prince. Give me your love as well.

SOPHIA You had it long ago. What good will it do you? No, it's bound to turn to harm. My father will start thinking. He's bound to think it out, given time enough and solitude. If I didn't faint for love of Mr. Blifil, it's not likely

it was for love of Mr. Thwackum. He'll work it out,
Mr. Jones, by a mathematical certainty.

TOM If we've to wait for his mathematics, we've a moment
yet.

SOPHIA Besides I love him, and I do believe a quarrel between
us would break his heart. And he's right when he says
I owe him duty as well as affection.

TOM He has no right to condemn you to misery all your life.
Now please, please, if he insists, if he overbears you,
don't stay here. Escape, come away with me.

SOPHIA Mr. Jones!

TOM I would escort you to any friends of yours who would
care for you. In honour and respectability.

SOPHIA I have friends in London.

TOM We could go there. You could—

WESTERN (off) Tom Jones!

SOPHIA No.

WESTERN (off) Jones! Jones! Tom Jones!

(SQUIRE WESTERN, *in a towering rage, bursts in and sees
that* TOM *is holding* SOPHIA's *hand.*)

You stand off that girl. Stand away! So it be you. Come
to my house as my friend and to be stealing my daughter out under my nose. Aye and you, miss, fainting for
Blifil, was it, and kissing and cuddling to get round me,
then. Tell ee, whoever thee be'st fainting for, or to be
pining for, art marrying Blifil! Set thy heart on a
bastard, hast ee? I tell ee, art marrying Blifil tomorrow,
if I have to whip you every step to the altar. So. Now.
Up to thy room this instant. Honour!

(HONOUR *comes in* D.L.)

HONOUR Sir?

WESTERN Go with thy mistress. When she's in her room, lock the
door, and bring I the key.

SOPHIA Father!

TOM Sir!

WESTERN Don't ee be fathering me. And don't ee be fainting till
upstairs wi't bed handy. Art staying there, to bread
and water, till thy duty comes back to thy mind. There!
Off! Go!

(SOPHIA *goes off* D.L. HONOUR *crosses and picks up the chair.*)

Honour.

HONOUR Sir?

WESTERN The key. Two minutes, or I'll skin thy backside.

HONOUR Sir.

(HONOUR *runs off after* SOPHIA, *carrying the chair.*)

WESTERN And now, bastard—

(TOM *puts up his hand and* WESTERN *is frozen in mid-denouncement as* TOM *turns quickly to the audience.*)

TOM But most of that interview is unsuitable for mixed company. It ended in his going to Squire Allworthy.

(SQUIRE ALLWORTHY *comes on through the hallway from L. and sits in his chair at the table, with his head bowed.*)

And laying a formal complaint that I had tried to seduce his daughter.

(TOM *crosses to stand D.R.* WESTERN *moves over to stand L. of the table. The downstage lighting fades and a spot comes up on* ALLWORTHY, *slightly illuminating the space all round the table, so there is a little light on* WESTERN *and—in a moment—on* THWACKUM *and* BLIFIL *when they come in.* TOM *is in shadow.*)

WESTERN It's what comes of breeding up a bastard like a gentleman and letting un come about to volks' houses.

TOM Other voices joined his.

(THWACKUM *and* BLIFIL *come in from the L. through the hallway and join* WESTERN. TOM *turns upstage towards* ALLWORTHY.)

THWACKUM He sold his horse for money to buy and corrupt poor Molly Seagrim.

BLIFIL I pray that you will forgive what my duty forces me to tell: on the day when you were near dying, he drank and sang and roared and filled the house with debauchery.

WESTERN Get my hands on him, I'll teach the son of a whore to meddle with meat for his master.

THWACKUM He went from your bedside into the arms of a village slut.

WESTERN He shan't ever have a morsel of meat of mine, or a varden to buy ut: if she will ha'un, one smock shall be her portion.

BLIFIL I hope he may have repented by now of the beating he gave to Mr. Thwackum.

WESTERN Son of a bitch were always good at finding a hare sitting: I little thought what puss he was after.

THWACKUM What parent can rest easy—

WESTERN My only child, my poor Sophy, that was the joy of my heart, and the hope and comfort of my age.

BLIFIL What woman is safe—

WESTERN I'll turn her out of doors. She shall beg, and starve and rot in the streets.

THWACKUM Compact of all vices—

WESTERN I loved him for a sportsman, and he were poaching my daughter.

BLIFIL I can forgive all save his ingratitude to you, my uncle.

THWACKUM Vice—

BLIFIL Ingratitude—

THWACKUM Drunken bestiality—

ALLWORTHY That will do!

(WESTERN, THWACKUM *and* BLIFIL *go. The study lighting comes up.* ALLWORTHY *takes a paper from the table drawer and turns to face* TOM.)

I have forgiven and forgiven and forgiven again, faults which I thought came from youth and wildness of spirits. In all your wrongdoing I credited you with honour and generosity. I was deceived, and my blindness has brought my neighbour near to ruin. You have ill-treated and abused a foster-brother who has shown nothing but tenderness and honour towards you. I can forgive your ingratitude to me, your lack of human tenderness and affection, but as I am landowner and magistrate in this parish, I cannot continue to foster and support corruption and vice. Take this paper. In it is enough to set you in an honest course of living, when you have found another home. If you squander it do not come to me for more. You are to leave at once, and never again to approach me for any reason.

(TOM *takes the paper, unable to speak.* ALLWORTHY *goes upstairs and into his bedroom. The study lighting fades and the out-of-door lighting comes up to show a moonlight night.* MOLLY *appears D.R.*)

MOLLY There. Oh master Tom, I be right sorry for ee. Turned out of doors, are ee? Naught but the clothes on your back? Nay then, wouldst come home along of me?
(TOM *shakes his head.*)
For the night, twould be for love, I'd not ask from ee. (*He shakes his head again.*)
Hast naught but the clothes on thy back?

TOM No. He gave me this. (*He holds up the paper, which he is holding loosely in his left hand.*)

MOLLY Where wilt go then? What wilt do?

TOM I'm not to see Sophia nor Mr. Allworthy again. Where can my comfort lie?

MOLLY Be hearty though. There'll be others to your liking.

TOM Who needs me now?

MOLLY Are you so poor as to go for a soldier?

TOM Soldier? Aye. There's need of soldiers up north, with the Young Pretender on the march.

MOLLY Oh my dear gentleman, and you'll likely be killed. Wilt give us a kiss in parting?
(*With his right hand* TOM *caresses her head and her shoulder, while she abstracts the paper from his left. Then he turns and goes out* U.R.)
Goodbye then, my dear heart. (*She comes D.R. Just before she disappears, she pauses and opens the paper.*)
Five hundred pounds! (*She goes off D.R.*)

CURTAIN

ACT II Interlude at Upton

The scene is the Lion Inn, Upton-on-Severn. The tapestry has been removed. The bottom flight of stairs has been moved round so that it now leads from R. to L. up towards the half landing. Just above the D.L. entry is a fireplace with the red glow of a fire shining from it and two candles burning on the mantelpiece. Under the half-landing and at right angles to the fire is a settle. Between the settle and the fireplace is a stool or small table and to the R. of the settle is another small table with four lighted candles on it. D.C. is a Windsor arm-chair, facing towards the fireplace. This area, entered through the hallway from the R., is the inn parlour. Hanging from the post which is farthest upstage is the inn sign. The groundrow shows a country scene, less wooded than in Act I. The bed in the visible bedroom has its head to the R., and its hangings have been changed. The parlour, stairs, landing and visible bedroom are all lit brightly enough for comedy-playing, and this lighting does not change as the candles are carried around. D.R. is in darkness and the cyclorama shows a moon-light night. Towards the end of the act day begins to break.

SUSAN, the inn maid, is on her knees, scrubbing the floor of the parlour. She is as dirty and slatternly as MOLLY, but not so cheerful. She is muttering to herself, and parts of this speech should be used by her again later in the act, as she moves about the stage on her various errands.

SUSAN And so what if it has got to be done, and is it always me to be doing it? 'Scrub the floor,' she says, 'and just get it sanded afore you go to bed.' Scrub the floor, and there's a lot of bed I'll see tonight. Wait here, wait there, run and fetch and carry, up stairs and down stairs, all day long and all evening, and then wait till the customers is gone and it's scrub the floor, ready for morning. And she's gone to her bed, and he's gone to his bed, and Bill and George and Harry gone to their beds

and ostler dead drunk asleep in the stable, and there's
me working still, fingers to the bone all night long,
scrubbing, cleaning, sanding, wash the glasses, polish
the tankards, wipe the tables, make the beds, sweep the
yard, feed the cat, never no rest, night nor morning,
year's end to year's end, dead on my feet and who's
to care when I'm done and buried and never a moment's
fun.

(While SUSAN *has been mumbling* TOM JONES *has en-*
tered from R., through the hallway, with MRS. WATERS.
She is a very pretty woman in her mid-thirties. Her
hair is dishevelled and she is wrapped in TOM's *cloak.*
He is carrying two bundles of clothes—hers and his
own. He helps her into the inn parlour.)

TOM   In there then, and we'll see if they're not all dead.
Hallo there!

*(*SUSAN *rises, her eyes travelling from* TOM's *feet to his*
face.)

SUSAN And you mind your muddy boots on my clean—
(She has seen TOM *and goes on without pausing for*
breath.) oh sir, what can I do for you?

TOM   Two rooms, er—?

SUSAN Susan, sir. Directly, sir.

TOM   And Susan, some cordial while you get them ready. This
lady has been attacked, and is still faint with the shock
of it. Here now, come and sit over here.

(He takes MRS. WATERS *over to the settle and seats her*
at the end nearest to the fire.)

SUSAN Attacked, sir? In Upton, sir?

TOM   No Susan, on her way here. Now quick with the cordial.

SUSAN Directly, sir. Two glasses, sir?

TOM   Two glasses, Susan.

SUSAN Was you attacked too, sir?

TOM   You get the cordial.

SUSAN Yes, sir, directly, sir.
(She goes off D.L.)

TOM   There now, how are you now?

MRS. WATERS Much better, sir. *(She gets up and stands with her back*
to the fire, letting the cloak fall back from her shoulders.

She is wearing formidable and impregnable corsets and a shift, with pantalettes beneath, and a few tatters of a dress.) I'm safe so I must soon be well.

TOM There's nothing you could put on in your bundle?

MRS. WATERS No. My baggage has gone before me to Bath.
(SUSAN *returns with a tray carrying two glasses and a decanter.)*

SUSAN Cordial, sir. *(She puts the tray down beside the candles on the table.)*

TOM Thank you, Susan, thank you.

MRS. WATERS Susan.

SUSAN Yes, mum?

MRS. WATERS The man who attacked me tore my dress past all wearing. Do you think you might find another for me?
(SUSAN *looks doubtful.* MRS. WATERS *holds up a guinea.* SUSAN *takes it and nods.)*

SUSAN My mistress' daughter is about your height. I'll see what I can get without waking her.

MRS. WATERS Thank you.
(SUSAN *picks up a candle and goes upstairs into the visible bedroom, where she turns down the bed. Then she carries the candle out and goes along the landing into the wings.)*

TOM There. This should help.
(MRS. WATERS *sits on the settle again.* TOM *pours two glasses of cordial and gives her one.)*

MRS. WATERS Thank you. And thank you for saving my life.

TOM I'd have saved a dog from strangling. Saving you was all pleasure and no pains at all. *(He sits at the right-hand end of the settle.)*
Tell me: what is your name.

MRS. WATERS Mrs. Waters. Jenny Waters. And yours?

TOM Tom Jones. And your husband?

MRS. WATERS A soldier. He has gone north to fight the Pretender. I went with him as far as Worcester before turning back.

TOM But who was with you? It was a soldier who attacked you. How came you to be alone with him?
(MRS. WATERS *puts her glass down on the stool to her* **left.)**

MRS. WATERS   I can feel his hands still around my throat! And your head? Your poor head!

TOM   That was nothing.

MRS. WATERS   A blow on the head is never nothing. Come, let me see.

(She bends his head down on to her bosom, and searches his hair for bruises.)

Oh, the poor head! There, it is hurt.

TOM   It's nothing.

MRS. WATERS   It's a nasty lump. Any dizziness? Any ringing in the ears?

TOM   Nothing, really.

MRS. WATERS   And the poor knuckles bruised. Mr. Jones, you are my preserver. I can never repay you, but I wish there were some way of proving my gratitude.

(SUSAN appears on the landing, carrying a dress, and begins to come down the stairs. TOM gets up.)

TOM   Another glass of cordial?

MRS. WATERS   Thank you.

(She gives him her glass and gets up too, crossing below him as he pours the cordial so that she is right of him when he gives her her glass.)

It has warmed me. I'm aglow all over.

TOM   Here you are then.

MRS. WATERS   Thank you. And you too?

TOM   Yes, indeed.

SUSAN   Dress, mum. *(She shoves it between TOM and MRS. WATERS, who takes it.)*

MRS. WATERS   Thank you. Now, that is my things and that is Mr. Jones's. Will you take them up for us?

SUSAN   You'll need some help.

MRS. WATERS   Thank you, I can manage. I'm sure it will fit charmingly. And Susan.

SUSAN   Yes?

MRS. WATERS   Mr. Jones must be kept warm after his exertions. Put an extra blanket on his bed.

SUSAN   Yes, mum.

(She takes the bundles upstairs, drops MRS. WATERS' on her bed and disappears along the landing into the wings

with the other. MRS. WATERS *puts the dress over the Windsor chair.*)

MRS. WATERS Could you hold this? (*She gives* TOM *her glass, and takes his cloak right off.*) And I give again your lendings, with my gratitude. (*She gives him the cloak, which he drops on the settle.*) Now, let's see. (*She slips out of the rags of her own dress, and into the one* SUSAN *gave her.*) The girl must be about my height, though 'tis but a drab, stuff thing. And no kerchief for my modesty—but there, what's to hide that you've not seen already. And forgotten like a gentleman, I trust. Thank you, Mr Jones. (*She takes her glass from him.*) To your health, and all you desire.

TOM And what more desirable—

MRS. WATERS Now Mr. Jones, country villages should not breed gallantry.

TOM There is no gallantry.

MRS. WATERS Why then, we make a pretty pair. I warrant, though you be young, there's many a maiden sighed for you already. Come now. Do me up, and don't protest you never did a dress up before.
(*She gives him her glass. He sets them both down on the tray, and starts to fasten her dress.*)

TOM No, madam. But there's more pleasure to be undoing them.

MRS. WATERS Fie for shame. Your hands are quick and skilful. This girl has a true country waist. I shall look a fatwife indeed. My, what hands you have.
(*His doing up of the dress ends in a kiss.* SUSAN *comes to the half landing and waits until they have finished. When they notice her neither of them is embarrassed.*)
And what less can I give in thanks to my preserver? Come then, Susan, may we to our rooms?

SUSAN Yes, mum. Up here, mum.
(*They follow* SUSAN *upstairs,* TOM *taking his cloak with him, and* MRS. WATERS *a candle.*)
This be for you, mum.

MRS. WATERS Thank you. And goodnight to you, Mr. Jones.

(She gives him her hand, which he kisses.)

TOM   I hope you sleep well.

MRS. WATERS   Do you fear I may be disturbed?

TOM   That might happen.

MRS. WATERS   Ah well. We must take what comes to us, in a country inn.

(She goes into the visible bedroom and takes off her dress and shoes. She gets into bed. As soon as she is in the bedroom, SUSAN *has shut the door and turned to* TOM.)

SUSAN   Your room's down there. *(Indicating offstage* L.)

TOM   Thank you, Susan.

SUSAN   Want me to come? To show you?

TOM   At the end, is it?

SUSAN   Yes.

TOM   No need then. There's for your pains. *(He slips a small coin into her hand, takes her candle, puts his hand under her chin and kisses her.)*

SUSAN   Sir!

TOM   Goodnight. *(He goes out along the landing.)*

SUSAN   If you want me in the night, I'm just down there!

TOM   *(off)* Thank you.

*(*SUSAN *comes downstairs, picks up her scrubbing brush and sinks into a dream.* SOPHIA *and* HONOUR *come in* U.R.)

SOPHIA   Yes, for a few hours we can rest. We have a good start on my father.

HONOUR   If we can wake anyone, and if they'll take us in, this hour of the night, ma'am.

SOPHIA   We can but try.

(They come through the hallway into the parlour.)

Hallo! Hallo! Mistress!

SUSAN   *(coming to with a jerk)* Sir? Ma'am. Oh. Was it for a room?

SOPHIA   If you please, yes. And we wish to be off early in the morning. As soon as it's light.

SUSAN   Well, I don't know, ma'am, it ain't usual to take—

SOPHIA   Here. There's an earnest of our honesty. *(She gives* SUSAN *a guinea.)*

SUSAN Oh, ma'am! This way, ma'am. Take your baggage, ma'am. Up here, mum. In here, I hope this will suit you, mum. (*She takes a candle and shows them up into the room opening off the half-landing. After a moment she reappears, having left the candle in the room.*) Thank you, mum. Goodnight. Goodnight.
(*She comes downstairs into the parlour and is about to start scrubbing again.* MRS. FITZPATRICK *and her maid* BETTY *come in U.R., carrying luggage and in a state of fright and hurry.*)

BETTY This way, Mrs. Fitzpatrick?

MRS. FITZ-
PATRICK Yes. In here. Quickly.

BETTY But if Mr. Fitzpatrick were to catch us—

MRS. F. Though my husband be at my very heels, yet for a few hours I must rest. Ho there! Girl! At once!

SUSAN Directly, mum. Was it for a room?

MRS. F. What else would it be, this time of night? Now here's a guinea for yourself, and we want to go directly to bed. I'm half dead with jouncing up and down in the oldest equipage in christendom, and your ostler is stone drunk and kept us standing about in the cold till I'm gone beyond pain and out of all reason. Now please, do give us a bed and quickly.

SUSAN Yes, mum, this moment, mum. (*She picks up the candle and leads them upstairs and into the bedroom at the head of the staircase, going in herself to light a candle inside for them.*)

MRS. F. And we've to be off as soon as it's light, so please to see we're called and the ostler sober.

SUSAN Yes, mum, in here, mum. I hope this'll do, mum, you did oughter be comfortable here. Goodnight then, mum. Goodnight.
(*She comes downstairs, muttering, sets her candle down on the table, and starts to scrub again.* TOM, *wearing a replica of his original shirt, but one which reaches his knees, comes quietly along the landing and into* MRS. WATERS' *bedroom, apparently locking the door. She is in bed and welcomes him in beside her. He*

gets into bed from the upstage side. They draw the sheets over their heads and remain absolutely motionless and without a sound of any kind. CAPTAIN FITZPATRICK *comes quickly on U.R., through the hallway and into the parlour. When he speaks he does so in a half whisper but with great urgency. He is a tall, powerfully-built Irishman.*)

CAPTAIN
FITZPATRICK   Ho there! Anyone here?
              (SUSAN *begins to get grudgingly to her feet. He grabs her by her neckerchief and lifts her up.*)
              You there now. Wake up now, will you?

SUSAN   Ow! Sir!

FITZPATRICK   Hush, then. It's only me. It's Captain Fitzpatrick, an officer and a gentleman. Don't be waking the household. Here now. Here's a handful of guineas, all to yourself. Now tell me, tell me true. I've lost my wife and come running to take her. On my soul, I've been near catching her already in two or three places, and found her gone when I caught up with her. Now if she be here, just carry me up in the dark and show her to me. Eh now? Will you do it? Quick now.

SUSAN   What would she be like then, your lady?

FITZPATRICK   Shorter than me, with a lot of hair. She's Mrs. Fitzpatrick. Might have been travelling with a gentleman. MacLachlan, damn his eyes.

SUSAN   Oh her.

FITZPATRICK   She's here?

SUSAN   Upstairs and first on your left.

FITZPATRICK   By God, you'll be scrubbing up blood in the morning!
              (*He rushes upstairs.* SUSAN *follows to watch him go and nearly falls over the table with the drinks tray on it. Shrugging, she picks up the tray and* MRS. WATERS' *abandoned dress and goes out D.L. Meanwhile* CAPTAIN FITZPATRICK *tries* MRS. WATERS' *door and finds it locked. He thunders on it and then bursts through, falling flat on the floor. There is a commotion under the bedclothes.*)
              Out of there, you whore! Harlot! Tis your husband

come with the Almighty to back him! (*He picks himself up, draws his sword and beats the bedclothes with
the flat of it.*) Out of there and I'll kill you. Both on
you now and I'll cut your throats. Show your face, you
painted Jezebel!
(*He seizes the bedclothes to pull them down.* MRS.
WATERS *holds them up and there is a tug of war while
she screams.*)

MRS. WATERS Help! Help! Rape! Help, someone! Rape! Villains!
Help, somebody, help!

FITZPATRICK And come out from the bedclothes hiding your fancy
man! You. I'll split you like a pig!
(SOPHIA *appears on the half-landing and stands appalled,
watching what is happening.* CAPTAIN FITZPATRICK *pulls
the bedclothes right off the bed. The bed is empty
except for* MRS. WATERS, *who grabs a pillow to hide
behind.* TOM *emerges at the foot of the bed, and stands
in the doorway as a new arrival.*)

TOM Hold! Stop that! Leave her, sir!

MRS. WATERS Help! Rape! Somebody help!

FITZPATRICK Where's he gone? What have you done with him?
(*He drops his sword on the bed and launches himself
to throttle* MRS. WATERS. TOM *intervenes and holds him
off.* MRS. WATERS *continues to scream inarticulately
until* CAPTAIN FITZPATRICK *ceases to try to get at her.*)

TOM No, sir, no! Are you drunk to frighten a lady?

FITZPATRICK It's my wife with a man and him not here. I'll kill her!
I'll kill her! I'll kill her! Let me go, I'll kill— I'll— I'll—
God Almighty, it's not my wife at all! (*He has pulled
the pillow away from her face.*)

TOM Are you drunk?

FITZPATRICK You've never seen me that. I'm Captain Fitzpatrick, sir,
a soldier and a man of honour. My wife's run off with
a man and I'm out to bring her home to my love and
I'll kill the pair of them. The girl was saying she was
here, but it's not you. You're not my wife.

MRS. WATERS No, I'm not, I thank God. And things are to a pretty
pass when an honest, virtuous gentlewoman cannot
travel her native land without strangers and savages

bursting into her room with nothing on, frightening her near to death and making her die of the cold.

FITZPATRICK Your pardon, ma'am. I'll be after putting the covers back.

MRS. WATERS Don't you touch me, you Irish savage!

(*He lifts the bedclothes and she takes them from him and holds them up under her chin.*)

TOM And for my part I apologise for coming like this. I was in bed, ma'am, when I heard your screams, and came to help you without sparing time to make myself fit to appear before a lady. I am most deeply sorry to have offended your modesty like this.

FITZPATRICK I can't understand it. I described Mrs Fitzpatrick to the girl, quite clearly I did.

TOM The best we can do, sir, is to retire and leave this good lady to her rest.

SOPHIA (*horrified*) Oh Tom! (*She returns quickly to her room.*)

FITZPATRICK True indeed, and I'm sorry again, ma'am. I'll be looking elsewhere to find her.

TOM Yes, along there. Goodnight then, ma'am, and I hope your rest is not disturbed again.

MRS. WATERS Goodnight, sir.

(TOM *closes* MRS. WATERS' *bedroom door and follows* CAPTAIN FITZPATRICK *along the landing and into the wings. As they go,* MRS. FITZPATRICK, *wearing her night-clothes, cautiously looks out of her room.*)

MRS. F. It is. It is. I knew it was, Betty.

(BETTY *joins her.*)

It's my husband. He's here. I knew it was his voice. Now quick. We must get dressed and packed and slip away before he finds us here. Quickly!

(*They go back into their room.* SUSAN *comes back into the parlour and begins to scrub the floor again.* TOM, *dressed still in the longer shirt, comes quietly along the landing and into* MRS. WATERS' *room. She greets him with laughter and again he gets into bed from the up-stage side: again they pull the sheets over their heads and again they remain absolutely motionless and without a sound of any sort.*)

SQUIRE WESTERN *comes in* U.R. *and through the hall-way into the parlour. He is carrying a horsewhip.*)

WESTERN Ah. There now, my girl. Still up then?

SUSAN I got to finish my floor, sir.

WESTERN You seen all them as come here tonight?

SUSAN Yessir. All on them, sir.

WESTERN Seen my daughter?

SUSAN I don't know, sir. I expect so.

WESTERN Sophy her name.

SUSAN None of them wasn't called by their given names, sir.

WESTERN Tall girl, that high. Pretty. Tiny waist. Hair. Might have been travelling with a young man.

SUSAN Oh her.

WESTERN You seen her?

SUSAN Yes.

WESTERN Where? Which room?

SUSAN I don't know as I ought to—
(*He gives her a coin.*)
—upstairs and first on your left.

WESTERN I'll kill him! I'll kill the pair on them!
(*He goes upstairs.* SUSAN *tries the water in the bucket with her hand.*)

SUSAN Stone cold and I'm freezing.
(*She picks the bucket up and goes out* D.L. WESTERN *thunders on* MRS. WATERS' *door.*)

WESTERN Jones! Tom Jones! You come out of there and I'll kill ee!
(TOM *springs out of bed, looks around for a hiding place and fails to find one. He rushes to the extreme right of the bedroom floor, looks out as through a window and notices the inn sign. He seizes it, swinging out to hang from it as* SQUIRE WESTERN *enters from the bedroom. After a moment he drops to the ground and huddles there, just under the window.*)
I'll kill ee, and as for ee, Sophy, I'll have ee home to bread and water and never so long as I live—why, who on God's earth be you, mum? What you doing in my Sophy's bed?

(MRS. WATERS *is beginning to scream. She thinks better of it.*)

MRS. WATERS   I might better ask who you are, to come bursting into a gentlewoman's bedroom to be frightening her half out of her wits. Is there to be no rest, no peace and tranquillity, this near to dawn, and everybody in their godly rest?

WESTERN   Mistress, ma'am, I do beg your pardon—

MRS. WATERS   And well you might. Your age, to be shouting and bursting in on a lady brandishing a horsewhip.

WESTERN   Aye, well I was like promised to find my daughter here.

MRS. WATERS   And a fine state of things when a man goes after his daughter with a horsewhip. What, are we savages? Are we barbarous Yorkshiremen to be horsewhipping our daughters? I tell you, sir, if you are for horsewhipping your daughter, no marvel she runs away from home, and heaven send you find her not.

(*By now* MRS. WATERS *is up on her knees on the bed, holding the bedclothes up in front of her, and driving* WESTERN *back step by step towards the door.*)

WESTERN   Tain't for my Sophy. Be for't young man—

MRS. WATERS   And lucky for her that she has a young man to care for her and take her away from a great drunken brute of a father who'll go bursting into inn bedrooms at dead of night. Out with you, sir, go out, out of my room!

WESTERN   Yes, ma'am. Pardon, ma'am.

MRS. WATERS   And if you can't be sober and peaceful, get back to Somerset, where they're all drunk and won't notice!

(WESTERN *withdraws, shutting the door behind him.* MRS. WATERS *goes to the window and waves to* TOM. *He makes several attempts to get back up through the window, with her leaning down over the head of the bed holding her hand out to help him.*

WESTERN, *after drawing breath for a moment on the landing, goes to* MRS. FITZPATRICK's *door and knocks.* BETTY *answers the door. He pokes his head past her to look inside the room.*)

WESTERN   Pardon, ma'am. No offence.

(*He withdraws his head and* BETTY *disappears.*)

Lord have mercy.

(*He turns to go down the landing.* CAPTAIN FITZPATRICK *appears and they meet. They seize on each other.*)

WESTERN Tom Jones?

FITZPATRICK MacLachlan?

(*They realise that they are not who they thought they were, and release each other.*)

WESTERN Oh. Pardon.

FITZPATRICK Oh. Pardon.

(WESTERN *goes down the corridor into the wings.* FITZ-PATRICK *comes down the stairs and out D.L.* TOM *has picked himself up and is trying to creep into the parlour when* CAPTAIN FITZPATRICK *comes downstairs, and* TOM *is frightened back into the yard. As soon as* CAPTAIN FITZPATRICK *has gone out,* SOPHIA *and* HONOUR, *dressed for travelling and carrying their bundles, creep out of their room and begin to tiptoe downstairs.*)

SOPHIA Hush, Honour, and quickly.

HONOUR How could he have caught us up so soon?

SOPHIA I don't know, but we both know his voice when we hear it.

(CAPTAIN FITZPATRICK *returns with* SUSAN *behind him. The sight of him paralyses* SOPHIA *and* HONOUR *at the foot of the stairs.*)

SUSAN To be sure I can't help you then, sir. Did you try all along that corridor?

FITZPATRICK That I did.

SUSAN Down the two steps and round the corner?

FITZPATRICK Yes.

SUSAN The room on your right at the top of the stairs?

FITZPATRICK That I did not—Harriet!

(*He has seen* SOPHIA, *and seizes her.*)

No. Hell. Saving your presence, ma'am. Beg pardon, ma'am. On the right, you said?

SUSAN Yes.

(*He goes up and into* SOPHIA's *room.* SOPHIA *and* HONOUR *come into the parlour.*)

SOPHIA Ssh, quietly, Susan, I beg of you.

SUSAN Trust me, ma'am, I'll not betray you.

SOPHIA The reckoning now.

SUSAN Aye, ma'am, just let me figure it.

(MRS. FITZPATRICK *and* BETTY *come out of their room, dressed for travelling and carrying their bundles.* SQUIRE WESTERN *reappears and grabs* MRS. FITZPATRICK *on the landing. At the sound of his voice* SOPHIA *and* HONOUR *shrink in horror on to the settle in the parlour.*)

WESTERN Sophy! Sophy! There! Oh. Asking your pardon, ma'am. (*He stands back to let them pass.* MRS. FITZPATRICK *sees the door of* SOPHIA's *room opening and dives into* MRS. WATERS' *room, with* BETTY *following her and shutting the door.* CAPTAIN FITZPATRICK *comes out of* SOPHIA's *room and meets* SQUIRE WESTERN *on the landing.*)

WESTERN Your servant, sir.

FITZPATRICK Servant, sir.

(WESTERN *goes into* SOPHIA's *bedroom.* CAPTAIN FITZPATRICK *goes into* MRS. FITZPATRICK's *bedroom.*)

MRS. F. (*to* MRS. WATERS) Thank you.

(MRS. FITZPATRICK *and* BETTY *come out of* MRS. WATERS' *room and downstairs.* MRS. WATERS, *despairing of sleep, gets up and begins to dress.* MRS. FITZPATRICK's *descent frightens* SOPHIA, *and when* MRS. FITZPATRICK *sees that there is someone in the parlour, she is also frightened.*)

SOPHIA No!

MRS. F. No!

MRS. F. Gracious heavens! Sophia Western!

SOPHIA Harriet Fitzpatrick!

(*They kiss each other on both cheeks.*)

SUSAN You ladies met before?

MRS. F. We were at school together. My dear creature, what are you doing here? Where are you going?

SOPHIA To London. I've run away from home.

MRS. F. And time too.

SOPHIA And you?

MRS. F. From my husband, my dear. And to London as well.

SOPHIA We can go together.

MRS. F. Indeed we can. (*To* SUSAN.) Here. This will answer the reckoning, will it not?

SUSAN Oh yes, ma'am. Thank you, ma'am.

SOPHIA And there's for me.
        (*As she pulls her purse out, her wallet falls to the floor.*)
        And Susan.

SUSAN   Yes, ma'am?

SOPHIA There is a—a gentleman passing the night here. With
        the lady above. A Mr. Tom Jones.

SUSAN   Yes, ma'am.

SOPHIA In the morning. When we are gone. Will you be so
        good? Give him this ring.

SUSAN   Yes, ma'am. And the message, ma'am?

SOPHIA No message. Just give him the ring.

SUSAN   Yes, ma'am.

MRS. F. Ha! I scent intrigue.

SOPHIA Quickly, Harriet. Let's be gone.

MRS. F. Indeed yes.
        (TOM *flattens himself in the shadow as they pass him,
        their hoods hiding their faces. They go through the hall-
        way and off U.R.*
        As they go, CAPTAIN FITZPATRICK *comes out of* MRS.
        FITZPATRICK's *room and* SQUIRE WESTERN *comes out of*
        SOPHIA's. *They meet on the landing.*)

FITZPATRICK Servant.

WESTERN Huh.
        (CAPTAIN FITZPATRICK *goes along the landing into the
        wings.* SQUIRE WESTERN *comes downstairs.*)
        Not here. I can't find un. Art sure her were here?

SUSAN   I don't know, sir. There's a young lady just left, sir.

WESTERN My Sophy? Were it my Sophy?

SUSAN   To be sure I never got her name, sir.

WESTERN How long ago? Which way did un go?

SUSAN   I'm sure I don't know. I got work to do, minding my
        own business. I can't be forever watching and seeing
        which way folks is off to this hour of the morning and
        my head never touched the pillow once, all night long,
        and my floor still not scrubbed.

WESTERN To London now, likely they'm to London.

SUSAN   Her was with her maid, weren't no young man with
        her.

WESTERN No?

SUSAN And her did say they was going to Worcester.

WESTERN Worcester.

SUSAN But me not having time to be standing in the road watching folk out of sight, I can't say which way she went, only which way she might have said she'd be going.

WESTERN Worcester. Aye, she'll be after meeting him there. I thank ee. (*Giving her money.*) And there's for ee. I'll be off then. Worcester. Aye and a waste of good hunting weather.

(*He goes out through the hallway and off U.R. As he goes,* MRS. WATERS *comes out of her bedroom, carrying her bundle.* CAPTAIN FITZPATRICK *comes back along the landing and they meet.* MRS. WATERS *drops her bundle.*)

MRS. WATERS Oh. Again you frighten me.

FITZPATRICK Most humble apologies. I'm not one for scaring the ladies. Not as a rule I'm not. You'll let me carry that.

MRS. WATERS Thank you.

(*They come down into the parlour.* SUSAN, *who has been counting her night's takings, hastily drops them back into her pocket.*)

FITZPATRICK She's not here. I'm after looking in every cranny, and there's more boots been thrown at my head this night.

MRS. WATERS Your wife?

FITZPATRICK Aye.

MRS. WATERS But how comes she to leave you?

FITZPATRICK I shall have satisfaction! I'll be running him through and through till his skin's good for bootlaces!

MRS. WATERS She ran from you to another man?

FITZPATRICK 'Tis the way with women.

MRS. WATERS Not with this one. Oh no. If my fate had brought me to marriage with a man like you, I'd never have seen another man thereafter.

FITZPATRICK You would not? Ah, but there's no accounting for some women.

MRS. WATERS Are you still following her?

FITZPATRICK Aye, she's headed for Bath, and I'll after and catch her there.

MRS. WATERS Bath? Heavens how strange!

FITZPATRICK Why strange? 'Tis a big city and we met while I was there.

MRS. WATERS No, only strange because that's where I was going.

FITZPATRICK Was going?

MRS. WATERS All my baggage is there. I sent it ahead. Only I was attacked and robbed yesterday, and escaped with little more than my life. Even this dress is borrowed. I look terrible.

FITZPATRICK There now, the tragedy. And I've to break in and disturb the little rest you were getting. Well now, you'll do me the honour to make amends.

MRS. WATERS Ah, you apologised. And sure you must be distracted. Though a woman who'd leave you can hardly be worth—

FITZPATRICK (to SUSAN) There, girl. That'll cover the reckoning here. (To MRS. WATERS.) You'll accept a lift in my coach.

MRS. WATERS Sir, my reputation. Travelling with a man so monstrously good-looking.

FITZPATRICK The devil with women's reputations. You'll come.

MRS. WATERS You're so masterful.
(They go out through the hallway and off U.R.)

SUSAN That poor young gentleman.
(TOM creeps in, shivering.)
Sir, you'll have your death.

TOM Oh Susan. Susan. It's not worth it. I'm young still but I must give it up. Oh, I'm so cold!

SUSAN I'll get your clothes. You'd like some mulled ale? Hot negus? (She is rubbing his hands and back as he stands before the fire.)

TOM Yes. Yes. Anything hot.

SUSAN There. We'll soon get you warm, you and me together. And you stay down here. That landing's wicked draughty. (She moves downstage.) And the night's not quite over. (She goes out D.L. TOM hops about from one foot to another, trying to get warm. He sees SOPHIA's wallet and picks it up.)

TOM What's this then? What? Dear heaven. It's Sophia's. It's her money, and she may be penniless. Susan! Susan!

(*He puts the wallet on the mantelpiece and rushes up-stairs and out of sight along the landing.* SUSAN *comes back with a steaming tankard.*)

SUSAN   Sir? Sir? (*She looks out into the yard.*) Where's he gone now? Ah, he's up to get dressed. There's modesty. As if I minded him with his britches off.

(TOM *comes rushing downstairs, wearing his trousers and shirt, and carrying the rest of his clothes.*)

TOM   Quick, Susan. There's a good girl. Help me to dress. Lend me a hand.

SUSAN   I don't want you dressed. There now, your ale'll be cold, and I put the poker in it, specially.

TOM   Boots, girl. Quick! Boots!

(*He sits in the Windsor chair and she helps him into them and then into his waistcoat and coat. She is beginning to get tearful, and grumbles half to herself.*)

SUSAN   And me been up all night with they comings and goings and my floor to scrub and them ruining it with trampling over what I just scrubbed, and the sanding to do, and then they'll be after me to be doing the breakfast and hot water here and hot water there. And never a touch of love or rest all night and what's the hurry for? If you'm after that Mrs. Waters, her's gone off with Captain Fitzpatrick, he's offered her a lift and I reckon her'll be paying in kind, and you didn't ought to be losing your heart to the likes of her, and you a fine young gentleman and her old enough to be your mother, take her in the right light of day.

TOM   No, I'm not after her. It's Miss Western—Miss Sophia Western who was here and dropped this.

(*He is dressed and has gone to the mantelpiece and picked up the pocket book.*)

Now tell me quickly. Was she bound for London?

SUSAN   Aye, she were too. Met Mrs. Fitzpatrick and went off together, friends from school.

TOM   Then she's run away for me. Mrs. Fitz—?

SUSAN   Fitzpatrick.

TOM   Fitzpatrick. I must catch her and give it her back, and thank you, Susan. (*He gives her a coin, kisses her quickly, picks up his cloak and bundle, and heads for the yard.*)

SUSAN Sir!

TOM Yes?

SUSAN She gave me something for you.

TOM Gave you? She knew I was here?

SUSAN There you are, sir. (*He drops the cloak and bundle and goes to her.*) She said Mr. Tom Jones, the gentleman as spent the night with that Mrs. Waters. (*She gives him the ring.*)

TOM She was here? She saw? After she left home for me?

SUSAN Sit down, sir.
(TOM *is oblivious of her.*)

TOM And she's alone. And penniless. And I am—Oh my Sophia!

SUSAN Drink your mulled ale.

TOM I can never get her now.

SUSAN Sir!
(*He hurries out through the hallway and off U.R.*)
Sir! Stay with me!
(*She is left in tears, with his ale in one hand and his coin in the other.*)

CURTAIN

ACT III   London

MRS. FITZPATRICK'S *house and the street outside it. The half-landing has been removed and the stairs now run in a single flight straight down towards the floats. What was* SOPHIA'S *door in Act II is now a window. The flat which contained* MRS. FITZPATRICK'S *door in Act II has been flown, revealing a large window behind it. The bed has new hangings and is as far upstage as possible. There is a small table with toilet articles on it to the right in the bedroom, and also a small chair or stool.*

Downstairs, in MRS FITZPATRICK'S *drawing-room, is a chaise longue, centre stage, with a small table at its head on the upstage side, and there is a light chair in the angle under the staircase. On the table is a book.*

The inn sign has gone, and two of the posts now have street lamps hanging from them. Between the hallway and the upstage pillar is a low chain, of the kind used to keep people off the grass. Between the downstage pillar and the downstage right tree flat, is a stone seat. Characters coming downstage from U.R. have therefore to come between the upstage pillar and the one next to it.

The D.R. tree flat has park railings in front of it so that the trees may be accounted part of a London park or square. The groundrow in front of the cyclorama shows a view of London, including St. Paul's.

On the right of the bedroom is a wooden structure—an upright and a crosspiece—which MRS. FITZPATRICK *can use as part of the frame of her window looking down on to the street, but which later becomes the crosspiece of the gallows.*

MRS. FITZPATRICK, *dressed to kill, is sitting in her bedroom, reading.*
TOM *enters D.R. wearing a cloak.*

> TOM   I could never get her now. Hopeless of winning Sophia
> back, cured forever of the tender passion, I hurried to
> London. I was bound to seek Sophia out, to return her
> wallet and assure her that, although forgiveness was out
> of the question, my reverent devotion to her would

keep me forever celibate. I knew no one in London, and hunted fruitlessly for weeks, until I was penniless as well as wretched.

(*A minuet begins, softly.* MRS. FITZPATRICK *puts down her book and comes downstairs.*)

At last, hungry and despairing, I found where Mrs. Fitzpatrick lived. I called on her.

(*He meets her at the bottom of the stairs. He bows and she curtsies. They begin to dance the minuet, but not closely*—TOM *is free to speak to the audience at appropriate moments during the dance.*)

I asked for Miss Western. She told me that Sophia had left her on reaching London, and gone to stay with relations. She had no idea where the relations might live, but entered most earnestly into my wish to find Miss Western and return her property. She promised to hunt for her, and invited me to call in the afternoon, to hear how she had succeeded. I called again—in the afternoon—and heard that she had not yet found Sophia. I called regularly, three times a week—in the afternoon—and Sophia had never been found.

(ANDREWS, MRS. FITZPATRICK'S *manservant, enters from the L. through the hallway.*)

Meanwhile, my own financial difficulties had disappeared.

(*He opens his cloak and* ANDREWS, *standing behind him, takes it off his shoulders and goes out, through the hallway and off L.* TOM *is now expensively and elegantly dressed.*)

And, but for the delay in finding Sophia, I found London society stimulating. Mrs. Fitzpatrick searched high, Mrs. Fitzpatrick searched low, Mrs. Fitzpatrick enquired of all her acquaintances, but Sophia was nowhere to be found.

Mrs. Fitzpatrick was desolated, I was in despair. As best we could, we consoled each other.

(*The dance ends in a kiss. Then she goes upstairs and along the landing into the wings. He turns back to the audience. The music stops.*)

But there came a day when I was not able to go to see Mrs. Fitzpatrick in the afternoon. I hurried round, therefore, in the morning, to make my excuses. The servant showed me into the drawing-room. Mrs. Fitzpatrick was out, he thought, but I could wait her return. I sat down, and I waited.

(*He takes the book from the table and sits down on the chair, reading.* SOPHIA *comes along the landing from the wings, down the stairs and goes to the table without noticing* TOM, *who gets up as he sees her. Not finding the book on the table, she looks round, and sees him. They look at each other speechlessly for a moment, and then she begins to sway slightly. He comes to her and seats her on the chaise longue.*)

Here, sit here, Sophia, sit down! I wouldn't for a moment have upset you like this. I have hunted for you, through the whole of London, but I wouldn't for the world have surprised you in this way. Except that I have found you at last and that is worth all the world in itself. After such a long, despairing search for you.

SOPHIA   You have been looking for me?

TOM   Yes. All these weeks.

SOPHIA   Why, Mr. Jones? What business could you have with me?

TOM   No, it's not to ask you to take my ring again—I've got it still, (*Feeling in his pockets.*) it's somewhere—here. I can never ask you to do that again. I know what has happened—what happened at Upton—has made it impossible for me ever to ask that again. I can't ask your pardon for that. It was past excusing.

SOPHIA   A night when I was homeless, partly for your sake.

TOM   When I was going north, hoping to save you from any further concern about me.

SOPHIA   Going north?

TOM   To the fighting.

SOPHIA   You lost your way?

TOM   I changed my mind. For good reason. You will see that I had good reason. But. As for that night at Upton. I want you to know, if I am never to see you again, at

least this much. It was evil, it was wrong past all that I
can say, but there was no love in it. I rescued her from
attack. The violence of her gratitude made her forward
a little, I think. And I was drunk with despair. There
was no love. Nothing of what I felt for you in it. I never
saw her before and I've never seen her since that night.
I don't know where she went. As soon as I knew
you had been there, I rushed away and came after you.

SOPHIA To London.

TOM Not to ask your forgiveness. I feared you might be
penniless, and this gave me an excuse for seeing you
once more in all my life. (*He brings out the pocket book
and gives it to her.*)

SOPHIA My pocket book!

TOM And the money still there.

SOPHIA Thank you.

TOM I was afraid you might be in some straits without it.

SOPHIA Oh, no. Living with Mrs. Fitzpatrick I have been well
looked after.

TOM Living here!

SOPHIA She's been so kind. We were at school together.

TOM Kind indeed. I was a little worried, coming this morning, that it might have been inconvenient. I had thought
of delaying it till the afternoon.

SOPHIA No, I am always out in the afternoon.

TOM Thank heaven I came this morning then.

SOPHIA Mrs. Fitzpatrick would have given me the pocket book.

TOM And so I would never have seen you again.

SOPHIA You are well lodged in London?

TOM Yes. And you? Your father? Does he still insist that
you marry Blifil?

SOPHIA Yes. He chased me a little beyond Upton and lost me.
When he found I was here, with a woman of good
reputation, he left me in peace for a while. But—oh
Tom, I fear he will be in London soon, and Blifil with
him.

TOM You won't marry Blifil.

SOPHIA No. But Tom, although I will not marry a man I hate,
neither can I marry against my father's consent. It

          would be wrong. I am sure of that in my own heart, and Mrs. Fitzpatrick agrees with me.

TOM   Does she then. (*He gets up and moves away from her.*) I couldn't ever ask you to marry against your conscience and certainly I could never ask you to marry me, as it is now, when I can only offer you ruin and suffering. (SOPHIA *goes to him.*)

SOPHIA   That's not the barrier. You have known for a long time that but for my duty to my father, I would rather have ruin with you than a fortune with anyone else. (*They fall into each other's arms for a moment.*)

TOM   No. You must obey your conscience and I must go away. I mustn't see you again. I must go right away. Only, please, keep this for me, this ring, so that I know you have something to remember me by.

SOPHIA   Yes.

    (*He puts the ring on her finger.* MRS. FITZPATRICK *comes along the landing from the wings and down the stairs, stopping a few steps up when she sees them together.* SOPHIA *sees her first, and then* TOM. *All three stand in confusion for a moment,* TOM *caught between the two women.* SOPHIA *is the first to recover.*)

    Why, Harriet. I thought you were gone out, or I would have had the servants call you. This gentleman found my pocket book that I spoke about, and has been kind enough to return it to me with the money in it.

TOM   Ever since I found it I have been looking for the lady whose name was written inside.

MRS. F.   Indeed, Sophia, you had very good luck that it fell into the hands of a gentleman of honour.

SOPHIA   But, sir, how did you find where I was living?

TOM   Luckily I had the help of a lady who knew you—distantly, by sight—and she spared no pains to help me in my search. But I must not keep you any longer—you will not be ready for your afternoon outing.

SOPHIA   I do thank you, sir, for spending so much pains on a perfect stranger.

TOM   No pains, Miss Western. If I may claim a reward, madam, it will be that I may be permitted to call again.

MRS. F. You are a gentleman, sir, and my doors are never shut
to people of fashion.

TOM Your humble servant, madam. Miss Western.

MRS. F. Good day.

SOPHIA Good day.

(TOM *throws the audience a sigh of relief and goes out
through the hallway and out U.R.*)

MRS. F. Upon my word, a pretty young fellow. (*She has moved
over, just R. of the chaise longue and waves, as if
through a window, at* TOM *as he goes off.*)
I wonder who he is.

SOPHIA Indeed, and so do I. I must say he behaved very hand-
somely.

MRS. F. And he is very handsome. Don't you think?

SOPHIA I didn't really notice. He seemed rather awkward in his
manner.

MRS. F. Yes, you're right. You can see, by his manner, that he
has not kept good company. Indeed, I almost question
whether he is a gentleman. I think I'll give orders not
to be at home to him.

SOPHIA Oh no indeed, after what he's done—besides, as you
said yourself, there was an elegance in his speech, a
delicacy, a way of expressing himself—

MRS. F. Oh, yes. He has a way of expressing himself. Sophia,
you must forgive me, indeed you must.

SOPHIA Forgive you?

MRS. F. You must indeed. For I had a horrible suspicion, when
I first came into the room—now you really must for-
give me, but for a moment I thought it must be your
Mr. Jones himself.

SOPHIA Mr. Jones? Whatever could make you think that?

MRS. F. I can't imagine. After all, he was well dressed.

SOPHIA I think it's a little cruel of you, Harriet, to be making
fun of me about Mr. Jones.

MRS. F. Not cruel, when you have promised me you never think
of him now. I shall begin to think your heart still
remembers him.

SOPHIA Oh, no. On my honour, I am as indifferent to Mr. Jones
as I am to that gentleman who just left us.

MRS. F. And on my honour I believe it. So let us leave it there
and never mention his name again. Dear creature!
(*They kiss.* MRS. FITZPATRICK *addresses the audience
behind* SOPHIA's *back.*)
Artful hussy!
(SOPHIA *goes to sit on the chair, reading the book
and looking at her ring,* MRS. FITZPATRICK *comes
downstage.*)
Now be careful, be careful, be careful. Clumsiness but
drives them into each other's arms. Now. Miss has
promised not to marry without father's consent. Father
is coming post-haste with Blifil, the pale country booby.
So long as the choice is between my Tom and booby,
Miss will be firm and father pig-headed. But. If I find
another suitor. Good-looking for Miss. Well-moneyed
for father. And once Miss is Missis, I'm safe with Tom.
'I didn't take much notice of him,' 'I wonder who he is.'
Oh, she must marry at once! A man of polish. A man
of tone. Lord Fellamar.
(*During the last lines of her speech,* LORD FELLAMAR *has
come in through the hallway, where he has been
received by* ANDREWS, *and as she says his name he
appears in the drawing room. He is the best-dressed
and also the most attractive man in the play—young,
good-looking and with a manner which is gentle but
entirely self-assured.*)

FELLAMAR Madam.

MRS. F. Lord Fellamar. I have been watching you. And indeed
I have had occasion to watch you, your visits have been
so common of late.

FELLAMAR And too long, you're going to say.

MRS. F. My dear sir, I have been happy, too happy, to feel that
you might form an attachment for Sophia.

FELLAMAR You would stand my friend?

MRS. F. Your friend indeed. And you wouldn't be doing badly,
for all she's the daughter of a Somerset fool of a squire.
She's an only child, and her father's estate is a good
three thousand a year. I think you would make her a
good husband.

FELLAMAR If she would make me her husband—

MRS. F. But she must be made to make you. Now, listen. You have a rival. No one you know. My dear sir, you know how it is in Somerset: nothing to do all day, surrounded by fresh air. (*Grimacing at the thought.*) Picking up romantic notions from every passing bird. Sophia gave her heart foolishly, childishly, before she was of an age to judge and before she had seen but one man, and he bound to ruin her. Now she feels pledged to him in honour and obstinacy. All her family can do has failed; her old father is like to die of spleen and sorrow. Oh, if only you could be the man to save her.

FELLAMAR But how? How can she be saved?

MRS. F. By a man. A man who is man enough to force what her obstinacy will not yield.

FELLAMAR Force? Are you saying—

MRS. F. Most of the servants will be out. Her own personal maid will be with me, out of earshot. If she will yield, well and good. If not, then for her sake be a man, and rescue her from lifelong shame, ruin and misery.

FELLAMAR Yes. I will.

MRS. F. Then, my dear Lord Fellamar. Go to her!
(*She turns him upstage towards* SOPHIA. *There is a burst of harpsichord music as he moves slowly upstage until he is standing upstage of the chaise longue. Meanwhile,* MRS. FITZPATRICK *goes quickly upstairs. On the landing she meets* HONOUR, *turns her round and disappears with her into the wings. As she disappears, the music stops and* LORD FELLAMAR *speaks to* SOPHIA.)

FELLAMAR Miss Western.

SOPHIA My lord!

FELLAMAR You weren't expecting me?

SOPHIA No. Did the servants not—

FELLAMAR I saw no servants.

SOPHIA Oh. I'll call Mrs. Fitzpatrick—

FELLAMAR She's out, my dear.

SOPHIA Oh.

FELLAMAR The house is empty.

SOPHIA I have to go out myself, directly.

FELLAMAR No.

SOPHIA You will excuse me—

FELLAMAR Are you afraid?

SOPHIA Sir?

FELLAMAR That I should be ungentle? (*He takes her hand.*)

SOPHIA Please—

FELLAMAR No. You're shaking.

SOPHIA You *are* frightening me.

FELLAMAR And your hand cold.

SOPHIA Let me go.

FELLAMAR Your hand in mine, how small it is. This was never made for fighting. One arm round you I can hold you: where's the point in fighting?

SOPHIA Please. Let me go.
You're shaking. I am to marry you, Sophia.

SOPHIA No! No!

FELLAMAR Let me in then, without a fight. It's soft, your cheek. Why fight when there is no victory, except in giving in? Gently then, gently, grant this for a keepsake. (*He slowly takes her kerchief and puts it in his pocket.*) There's honour and love, and long, slow happiness. There now. Give what I could take in a fight. (*He kisses her gently. She does not resist.*) Sweet. Sweet and be gentle. I'll teach you all the way, my heart, and that you forget your country boy.
(*He kisses her again, but the words 'country boy' have reminded her of* TOM, *and she breaks away from him.*)

SOPHIA No! Get off me! Leave me be!

FELLAMAR Come here.

SOPHIA No!
(*He catches her.*)

FELLAMAR You're as willing as any henwife might be. Cooped here, you're not one for a nunnery. Madam, you're mine by fair or by ill, and half your heart is in the ill, I think.

SOPHIA Let me go!

FELLAMAR Fight and I'm glad of it. It shows you haven't the habit yet. But fight with a design to lose. (*He picks her up and carries her upstairs.*) Raise the house then. Try. Try.

Nothing. No one. But me and your lost virtue out the door.

(*He throws her on the bed. As he does so,* WESTERN, ALLWORTHY *and* BLIFIL *come on U.C. and stand, R. of the hallway, knocking.*)

WESTERN Open up! Open then! Open this door! In, let me in!
(ANDREWS *comes through the hallway from L. and lets them in through the hallway into the drawing room.*) Where is she? Damn me, I'll unkennel her. Show me her chamber. Where's my daughter? Gone to ground? What have you done with my daughter?

ALLWORTHY Hush a minute.

WESTERN Why should I?
(*In the moment of comparative silence,* SOPHIA *gives a strangled scream.* WESTERN, ALLWORTHY *and* BLIFIL *rush upstairs.* ANDREWS *goes out L. through the hallway.*)
Sophy! Sophy!
(*He bursts into the bedroom and pulls* FELLAMAR *off* SOPHIA. ALLWORTHY *reaches in through the doorway, seizes* LORD FELLAMAR *and pulls him out on to the landing, where* BLIFIL *is keeping a careful distance from trouble.*)

ALLWORTHY Your name, sir?

FELLAMAR Leave go of me, sir. I am a gentleman.

ALLWORTHY You're a cheap scullion, sir, and off with you. (*He throws* LORD FELLAMAR *downstairs.*)

WESTERN Ah, but I've a word for un! (*He leaves* SOPHIA *and comes part way down the stairs.*) And you let be with my daughter.

FELLAMAR Mr. Western?

WESTERN Ah, and I'll have no man lay hands on my daughter.

FELLAMAR I mean honour, sir, I mean marriage.

WESTERN She's bespoke.

FELLAMAR I am wealthy, sir. I'm a good match.

WESTERN You're London scum.

FELLAMAR Sir, you cannot know my name.

WESTERN What is it then?

FELLAMAR I am Lord Fellamar.

WESTERN A lord?

FELLAMAR Yes.

WESTERN About the court?

FELLAMAR Yes.

WESTERN A Hanoverian. A Whig. You came here and you rape my daughter and you haven't even the grace to be a Tory! I tell you, sir, my daughter's bespoke. And you're a son of a bitch, for all your lace coat. Out and be damned to you!

FELLAMAR Sir, you offer me insults.

WESTERN I offer you nothing.

FELLAMAR I demand satisfaction.

WESTERN Be satisfied with no for an answer. Lout! Lord! Whig! (FELLAMAR *strikes* WESTERN, *who falls back roaring.* ALLWORTHY *rushes down between them and speaks to* FELLAMAR. BLIFIL *follows him down.*)

ALLWORTHY Outside, sir. There will be no fight got up between the two of you. Be thankful that for her sake we keep this story silent. Go now.

FELLAMAR Indeed I am going, sir. I see that country bumpkin is below my notice. I am sorry I dirtied my fingers with him. God, a fool, a drunk and a Tory. (*He goes out through the hallway and off* U.R. SOPHIA *has come to stand at the top of the stairs.* ALLWORTHY *turns to her.*)

ALLWORTHY Come now, my dear, all's well at last. Come down.

SOPHIA Father! (*She runs to* WESTERN, *avoiding* BLIFIL, *who is at the foot of the stairs ready to help her.*)

WESTERN There now. Ha't got a tousling. Nothing but that. Hey then, Sophy? Art well then? (*He sits her on the chaise longue.*) There now. There's with your fine ladies and staying in London. There's with your high manners. There's with running away from home. Tell ee, my girl, search all London, you'll not find one maid but yourself. And tha'rt a near miss now. This be London, the sink and cess-pit of the nation, and you'm finishing here, my girl, and to home where there's honour and kindness left, aye and bread and water too, till ee comes to thy senses.

ALLWORTHY Let her be now, sir. She's overwrought.

(WESTERN *takes his cloak off to put it round* SOPHIA's *shoulders.*)

WESTERN Aye, sha't come home with me, my pretty. We'm at the Hercules Pillars at Hyde Park Corner. And soon we'm to Somerset. Come then. Aye, Blifil, sha't have her, I promise ee.

ALLWORTHY Not unless she's willing. (*He turns to* BLIFIL.) And I say that particularly to you. There's to be no force or over-persuasion used. She must be freely willing. (*He goes out with* BLIFIL.)

WESTERN Willing? Aye, fair enough, neighbour. She'll be willing, if I've to twist both her arms off.

(*He follows with* SOPHIA. *They go through the hallway and off U.R. As they go,* TOM *comes on D.R.*)

TOM She was always my good angel, and the moment I set eyes on her, I felt hot with the thought of all that had passed between Mrs. Fitzpatrick and myself. I had stood, offering honourable love to an honourable woman, and I was the kept darling of a dishonourable woman. I could not bear to meet, to see, to talk to Mrs. Fitz-patrick again. My flesh crept to think of her. But to get rid of her? She had been kind to me. She had cared for me. I couldn't afford to return her presents. I must write. But not that I hated her. No, I could rely on her jealously-kept reputation. The one thing I knew she would find unbearable would be that the world should know her for a woman with a lover. I thought then to write such a letter as would make her be the one to put an end to our fellowship forever. Devilish clever, I was.

(*He goes out D.R. Offstage R.,* CAPTAIN FITZPATRICK *begins to sing and then comes on U.R., his arm round* MRS. WATERS' *waist. He sings the song straight through, regardless of interruptions. During the song, the* CON-STABLE *comes on U.R., looks at them suspiciously and then goes off D.R. There is a chink of money as some-one throws them some pennies from a nearby house.* MRS. WATERS *begins by trying to silence* CAPTAIN FITZ-

PATRICK, *interjecting remarks like,* 'Hush, you terrible man. In the streets! Hush. The Constable. Captain Fitzpatrick, the Constable.' *After the* CONSTABLE *has gone, she joins him and they finish the song as a duet.*)

FITZPATRICK 'Jenny is my only joy
Faithless as the winds or seas,
Sometimes wanton, sometimes coy,
Yet she never fails to please.
If with a frown,
I am cast down,
Jenny smiling,
And beguiling,
Makes me happier than before.'
(*See p. 96 for music.*)
So then, Jenny, we're here, and I must be telling you I'm sorry the journey's over.

MRS. WATERS Am I to be deserted then, as soon as we reach London?

FITZPATRICK No, faith, but the old nag lives just here. Now sit you down, and don't be for making eyes at passing strangers.

MRS. WATERS Will you be long?

FITZPATRICK A quarter of an hour. I married her fortune. If I'm cracking the golden eggs, 'tis but honest to give a nod to the goose.

MRS. WATERS That's not how you felt when you half killed me with fright at Upton.

FITZPATRICK My honour was at stake. Would you have a man forget his honour, and him a soldier? No. I'll kill the man I find her with!
(*He comes through the hallway into the drawing room.* MRS. WATERS *sits on the stone seat, facing upstage.*)
Mrs. Fitzpatrick! Mrs. Fitzpatrick!

MRS. F. (*off*) Yes? Who is there? (*She comes along the landing from the wings.*) Who is it, then, shouting and raising the roof when I've—gracious heavens, it's you!

FITZPATRICK Aye. Me.

MRS. F. Well, I'd have you know that this is a civilised country, and a civilised city, and a house with neighbours within earshot and servants that can't be bullied and kept in terror by the master and you can't be keeping your wife a prisoner here, frightening all the neighbours away and shouting and throwing things, and making wild accusations of God knows what outrages that never an innocent woman had to put up with since time began and forcing her to run away and endure heaven knows what torment and danger on the way to finding refuge in a civilised city where you can't be carrying on like that.

FITZPATRICK Are you done?

(MRS. FITZPATRICK *comes downstairs.*)

MRS. F. And what are you doing in London anyway?

FITZPATRICK Should a husband not visit his wife?

MRS. F. No. Not—not in a personal way.

FITZPATRICK Not personal? Wouldn't a loving wife, when her husband comes from a journey and a long absence, be glad if his joy overwhelmed him?

MRS. F. No.

FITZPATRICK Wouldn't a loving husband rush to the arms of his wife, throw her on the sofa— (*He throws her down on the chaise longue.*)

MRS. F. No.

FITZPATRICK And pleasure her before taking his boots off?

MRS. F. (*calmly—removing herself from his clutches*) No. Animal.

FITZPATRICK Then who's been to it with you?

MRS. F. No one. What do you mean, 'been to it'?

FITZPATRICK You know what I mean and I'll not be coarse in my speech and you a lady. If I'm not welcome, there's someone else. Now, who is he?

MRS. F. No one. I tell you. I'm no animal. I've my books. I've the theatre. *Le théâtre. L'opéra.* A sufficiency of elegant female acquaintance. A school friend staying with me —well, until but a little while, her father came to town and she went therefore to stay with him.

FITZPATRICK Aye, belike he didn't like the company she kept. Or was it the father? Did the girl go for that she saw how it was between you?

MRS. F. Mr. Fitzpatrick, you disgust me.

FITZPATRICK Mrs. Fitzpatrick, I know you of old. Why do you think

I came without notice? I'll be searching the house and there's not one bed I'll not look under.

MRS. F. You may do as you please.

(*He rushes up the stairs.* ANDREWS *comes in with a letter on a salver.*)

Oh. Thank you, Andrews.

(ANDREWS *goes.*)

FITZPATRICK And you may stay there, madam, and not be stirring to give warnings.

MRS. F. You need not think your coming will make me stir myself.

(CAPTAIN FITZPATRICK *goes into the bedroom, looks under the bed, and then goes along the landing into the wings.*)

Heavens be thanked he took no note of the letter. (*She opens it.*) Yes, it's Tom. The fool, I told him never to write. (*She reads from the letter.*)

'You, who know the inmost recesses of my soul, cannot have failed to remark the dejection and wildness of spirit which have of late darkened my whole existence. You must have divined that it is the secrecy, the furtiveness of our love which oppresses me. So great, so overwhelming is my passion that I can no longer bear that we should meet so little and in so backstairs a manner. Make me therefore, I entreat—nay, I insist— your open lover.' (*She is horrified.*) My open lover! 'Your open lover before all the world, that I may see and be with you every hour of the day and night.'

Villain. Villain. 'Until this is accomplished, my doubt, my jealousy—' Jealousy? That girl's at the bottom of this. 'My doubt, my jealousy, the fervour of my passion make me unfit for any company, even that of her in whom my whole happiness is lodged. I remain, ever my most admired, adored—' (*She is furious, but still coolly in control of herself.*) Low, treacherous, inconstant, ungrateful villain. So. He's had enough of me. He wants to end our relationship. He sits there, in the clothes I bought him, sucking the quill I gave him and devising treasons against me. 'My open lover'. Full well he knows I could never allow it. It's that girl. That teasing, sly, niminy miss. One sight of her, and he's done with me. Cast aside like the country clothes I took from him that first night. For that I am two, three, four years older than Miss Country Mouse. I could scratch his eyes out. Tear him to pieces. 'Jealousy, fervour, my open lover.' And if I would, as if I could have an open lover, with that Irish stout-bottle, (*Gesturing towards the bedrooms.*) ready to kill the very bugs in my bed. Aye. Aye. Now there's a thought. When a man seeks to deal double with a woman, he should walk wary, for 'tis as hard for a man to deal double as it is for a woman to be straight-forward.

(CAPTAIN FITZPATRICK *appears on the landing and comes down the stairs. Some loiterers appear in the street, chatting to each other and to* MRS. WATERS.)

FITZPATRICK Right then. You've beaten me this time. I'll own I found nothing. But I'll be back. I'm warning you, when you least—

MRS. F. (*going to him*) Oh, husband, husband! (*She bursts into tears.*) Husband, husband!

FITZPATRICK What's this for then? I told you, I found nothing.

MRS. F. It's the sight of you, the thought of you. Recalled me to my duty.

FITZPATRICK Duty?

MRS. F. As a wife. Oh husband, it is London society has infected me. And your long absence.

FITZPATRICK Where is he? Where've you put him? Where's he hidden? (*He makes for the stairs.*)

MRS. F. No, not in the house. Not just now.

FITZPATRICK Who is it? Where is he?

(*A woman with a basket crosses upstage.*)

MRS. F. Forgive me though. Forgive me and make me your wife again.

FITZPATRICK I'll forgive you when he's dead.

MRS. F. You will forgive me. If ever sincere repentance—

FITZPATRICK All right. After I've killed him. Give me his name.

(TOM *and* BLIFIL *appear U.R. They are deep in conversation and walk very slowly downstage.*)

MRS. F. A letter. From him this morning. (*She hands it to him.*)

FITZPATRICK (*looking at it*) Lodging in Bond Street. Tom.

MRS. F. Jones. Tom Jones. Lodging with Mrs. Miller in Bond Street.

FITZPATRICK Good then.

MRS. F. (*holding on to him*) But I pray you. Don't risk your life.

FITZPATRICK Risk? What risk? Isn't one from Ireland worth six here?

MRS. F. The coward's part is often best.

FITZPATRICK Who's a coward? Leave go!

MRS. F. No, look. Look. He's here.
(*They look, as if through a window, at* TOM *and* BLIFIL.)

FITZPATRICK Where?

MRS. F. There.

FITZPATRICK The one in black?

MRS. F. No, you fool, the proper man. The pretty one.

FITZPATRICK Pretty? I'll bring you his nose to supper.
(*He rushes out through the hallway and into the street.*
MRS. FITZPATRICK *runs upstairs to watch the fight
through her bedroom window. Servants enter, clear the
furniture through the hallway and off L., and close the
doors on the downstage side of the hallway, so that
it now looks like the outside wall of a house. Meanwhile*
CAPTAIN FITZPATRICK *has been fighting his way through
the little crowd which is blocking the gap between the
upstage pillar and the one next to it.* MRS. WATERS, *seeing that he is up to some violence, tries to detain him.
He does not get through the commotion to confront* TOM
until the furniture has been struck and the doors closed.
TOM, *expecting no evil, greets him in a friendly way.*)
Sir!

TOM Me, sir?

FITZPATRICK Aye, you, sir. D'you call yourself Tom Jones?

TOM I do, sir.

FITZPATRICK Live with Mrs. Miller to Bond Street?

TOM Yes, sir.

FITZPATRICK Then you're dead and there's to prove it.
(*He knocks* TOM *down and draws his sword.* TOM *draws
his sword as he gets up.*)

MRS. WATERS No, no. Tom! Both of you! No!

(TOM *and* CAPTAIN FITZPATRICK *fight. The woman with the basket returns, screams and stays to watch, milling about the fight with the rest of the crowd.* CAPTAIN FITZPATRICK *wounds* TOM *slightly, and then runs himself through on* TOM's *sword. As he falls,* TOM *drops his sword to help him.* MRS. WATERS *runs over to them.*)

BLIFIL The Watch! The Watch! A constable here!

MRS. WATERS Tom! Get away with you. Off now, quick!

TOM Mrs. Waters!

MRS. WATERS Don't stop to gape. He's dead for sure, and you to prison if you stay.

TOM I drew in defence.

(*The* CONSTABLE *pushes through the crowd.* BLIFIL *disappears U.R.*)

MRS. WATERS Don't stay! Too late.

(TOM *relinquishes* CAPTAIN FITZPATRICK *to* MRS. WATERS, *who checks quickly that he is dead and then leaves him lying, and stands up to meet the* CONSTABLE.)

TOM Constable, this man attacked me. I fear in defending myself, I have killed him.

CONSTABLE Ah well, sir, it comes to all of us. Gentlemen will be gentlemen and when gentlemen are gentlemen one of 'em generally ends up a dead gentleman. I shall have to ask you to come before the magistrate, sir.

TOM Yes, of course. Blifil—? (*He turns to look for him, but* BLIFIL *is not there.*)

CONSTABLE What, sir?

TOM My foster-brother. No matter. Mrs. Waters.

MRS. WATERS Yes?

TOM My foster-brother Mr. Blifil was here. He is seeking to reconcile me with Mr. Allworthy. Could you find him and tell him what has happened?

MRS. WATERS Where does he live?

TOM Hercules Pillars, Hyde Park Corner. Since it was self-defence, I should need no help, but I would have him know.

MRS. WATERS That he shall.

TOM Good then.

MRS. WATERS And I'll be to prison to see you.

TOM Thank you.

CONSTABLE Right, sir?

TOM Yes.

CONSTABLE Then if you'll excuse me, sir. 'Tis a little matter a mite embarrassing for me, sir, but if you wouldn't mind just slipping these on, sir. Just for the look of the thing. (*He manacles* TOM.) There then. Surprising these things, how they seem to fit all the gentry. Tell you, sir, there's been a royal duke worn them in his time. Come along then, sir, we'll soon have you snug and comfortable in the Gatehouse prison. Aye, you two! (*He speaks to two men remaining from the crowd.*)

FIRST
BYSTANDER Us?

CONSTABLE Aye, you. Follow along with the body, sharpish, and it's sixpence each on you.

FIRST
BYSTANDER Right, sir.
(*The* CONSTABLE *takes* TOM *off* D.R. *The* BYSTANDERS *move to the body, searching the pockets for money.* MRS. WATERS *begins to follow* TOM *and the* CONSTABLE, *but stops and returns to overhear the next scene when it starts.* BLIFIL *reappears* U.R., *and comes down to the two* BYSTANDERS, *speaking to them and to the woman with the basket.*)

BLIFIL Good-day to you both. And you, if you please.

FIRST
BYSTANDER Sir?

BLIFIL This is a terrible thing to happen. Fighting, murder in our streets. Thank heaven, there will be justice, a fair trial and a fair hanging.

FIRST
BYSTANDER Self-defence. Won't be no hanging.

BLIFIL Self-defence? Every time a gentleman is killed the gentleman killer is excused for self-defence. Would you get that treatment? No, my friends, you'd be hanged for an example. Is there to be no hanging of gentlemen? Are they never to be given an example? To be warned

from rioting in the streets? Come now. You are witnesses, and bound to be called at the trial. I think you
saw that the killer was the first to draw.

FIRST
BYSTANDER No, sir—

BLIFIL The killer was the first to draw. (*He slips money into
the hand of the* FIRST BYSTANDER.)

FIRST
BYSTANDER The killer was the first to draw, sir.
(BLIFIL *slips money to the* SECOND BYSTANDER.)

BLIFIL The killer was the first to draw.
(*The* SECOND BYSTANDER *chimes in halfway through*
BLIFIL'*s sentence.*)

SECOND
BYSTANDER First to draw, sir.

BLIFIL Good. As much again after the trial, if he hangs. Now,
quick with the body!
(*The* BYSTANDERS *pick up the body.*)

FIRST
BYSTANDER Legs.

SECOND
BYSTANDER Head.

FIRST
BYSTANDER Drag him, he's dead.
(*They drag the body out D.R. as* BLIFIL *turns to the
woman with the basket.*)

BLIFIL Now you.

WOMAN I wasn't there. Not at the beginning. I never saw how
it started.

BLIFIL I think you wrong yourself. I think you were here from
the beginning, and you saw the younger man draw on
the older. There's a dress for you and shoes for the
children, and more to come after the trial, if he hangs.

WOMAN Swear a man's life away? I don't know—

BLIFIL But I do. I was here at the start, and I'm telling you
how it started.

WOMAN Yes, sir.

BLIFIL So now you know.

WOMAN Yes, sir.

BLIFIL As if you'd been here.

WOMAN Yes, sir.

BLIFIL Then why not earn an honest penny saying so?

WOMAN I don't— Yes, sir.

BLIFIL The younger man drew on the older. (*He slips her a coin.*)

WOMAN The younger man drew on the older.

BLIFIL And as much again if he hangs.

WOMAN Sir.

(*She goes out D.R. BLIFIL comes downstage.*)

BLIFIL And it grieves me. But how else is Sophia to be made safe? Or my uncle's property? And surely such severity is love. To release him to heaven's mercy now, before longer life brings greater sin.

(*He goes out D.R. MRS. WATERS comes downstage.*)

MRS. WATERS Who was that? Why? Oh Tom, you're over ears in trouble.

(*She goes out D.R. MRS. FITZPATRICK gets up.*)

MRS. F. So, I'm a widow. (*She savours the idea.*) A widow. And black becomes me. He shall hang. I'll be a witness and he shall hang till the crows peck at the heart that loves Sophia. And as for Miss. What should a repentant, sorrowing friend do, but send Mr. Jones's letter straight to her!

(*She goes along the landing into the wings. As she goes, a flat painted to look like a wall comes down to hide the bedroom furniture, leaving enough of that level downstage for use as the scaffold. The D.R. tree flat pivots in, showing the corner of a prison cell. On the right-hand wall is a high, barred window. There is a three-legged stool on the floor of the truck, and beside it stands TOM. He is heavily manacled, at the ankles as well as the wrists, and is wearing a shirt and an old pair of breeches, worn and stained. He is holding a letter from SOPHIA, which he is reading, and also the letter he wrote to MRS. FITZPATRICK. The lighting fades to an amber glow through the bars on to the cell wall, and a spot on the D.R. area. TOM sinks to the ground in despair.*)

TOM No. Oh Sophia, no.

(*The* CONSTABLE *brings* MRS. WATERS *in* D.R., *and leaves her with* TOM. *She is still wearing her cloak, and carries a small basket with a cloth over it.*)

MRS. WATERS Tom? Tom my dear, sit up. There's nothing could be as bad as that.

TOM Please. Please to go away.

MRS. WATERS Not so likely, neither.

(*She brings the stool down and sits beside him.*)

I'm fitting to help you, seeing you saved my life and killed my encumbrance. Come now. Here's eggs and grapes—sickness or prison, the presents are always the same. Now my lad, I've hard news for you, but you've had it already, by the looks of you. What is it now? That man was so little use to the world he was hardly worth killing. What's cast you down?

TOM Sophia. Look. (*He gives her the letters.*)

MRS. WATERS Your Sophy? 'Letter from you to Mrs. Fitzpatrick. I am convinced it is in your own hand. All I desire is, that your name may never more be mentioned.' What letter? (*She looks at the other letter.*) Oh. Oho. So your right hand hath found what your left hand was doing.

TOM There's no joke. She has forg'ven and forgiven and forgiven. This is an end to it all.

MRS. WATERS Even forgiven me? I had hoped to escape forgiveness till I was forty, but there. I may buy a mob cap and learn to knit. Come now, Tom, be a man. When she wrote this, did she know you were in prison?

TOM No.

MRS. WATERS And to be tried for your life?

TOM No.

MRS. WATERS And maybe hanged? There's nothing wins a woman's heart like getting yourself killed.

TOM It would be best for us all if I were.

MRS. WATERS Hush. Not so loud. You might get your wish. Now then. Do you know, anywhere, of anyone who might have a grudge against you? Bitter and deep?

TOM Mr. Western?

MRS. WATERS No, not Mr. Western, I know him, he's not changed

since the days when he smacked my bottom. A man,
but young. Nearer your own age.

TOM (*showing little interest*) Young? No.

MRS. WATERS Well, there's someone. Bribing them as saw you fighting, to say you started the fight.

TOM Bribing them?

MRS. WATERS And if you started it, it's not self-defence, and if it's not
self-defence, it's a hanging matter, and you might get
your wish.

TOM But you'll speak for me.

MRS. WATERS One woman? And her for half a night your bedfellow?
No, Tom. There's danger here.

TOM And if so there be. Who's to hurt if I die?

MRS. WATERS Oh poor heart! Your Sophy for one. Now promise me
you'll not throw yourself in your tears to drown, and
I'll be round to Squire Allworthy's as soon as I can.

TOM He's from town.

MRS. WATERS I'll find him, or besiege his lodging till he's back.

TOM It will do me no good.

MRS. WATERS Mr. Allworthy's a merciful man.

TOM And just. You can't help me there.

MRS. WATERS Oh get along with your despair. You'll have me in tears
and all.
(*The* CONSTABLE *comes in D.R. and stands waiting to
take* MRS. WATERS *out.*)
Here. Eat your grapes and dry your eyes. There's things
to be told Mr. Allworthy, and there's me to be doing it.
(*She pushes the basket into his hands and goes out D.R.
followed by the* CONSTABLE. TOM *puts the basket down
on the truck and sits on the stool.* MRS. WATERS *comes
in again U.R. and comes down to centre stage, facing
the D.R. entrance, where* ALLWORTHY'S *servant appears.
Two more spots come up to light the two of them.*)
Mr. Allworthy, if you please.

MANSERVANT Mr. Allworthy is not here today.

MRS. WATERS Thank you. I'll come tomorrow.
(MRS. WATERS *and the* MANSERVANT *stand still as* TOM
speaks. He looks out front.)

TOM Two days, and they hold my trial.

(MRS. WATERS *speaks to the* MANSERVANT *again.*)

MRS. WATERS Mr. Allworthy, if you please.

MANSERVANT Not here today.

TOM One day, and my trial is here.

MRS. WATERS Mr. Allworthy, it's very urgent!

MANSERVANT Mr. Allworthy has gone to the country.

MRS. WATERS When will he be back?

MANSERVANT Next week, I believe.

MRS. WATERS Early next week?

MANSERVANT I'm sure I can't say.

(TOM *stands up.*)

TOM By my hand, my lord, but in self-defence.

MRS. WATERS Soon, it must be soon.

MANSERVANT I couldn't say.

(TOM *drops his head.*)

TOM In seven days they come for me.

MRS. WATERS He must come soon. He'll be too late.

TOM The days are short. (*He sits.*)

MRS. WATERS Oh soon!

(MR. ALLWORTHY *comes quickly in past the* MAN-SERVANT, *who bows and goes out. The lighting* D.L. *brightens and the light on* TOM *fades so that he is left almost in darkness.*)

Mr. Allworthy.

ALLWORTHY Yes?

MRS. WATERS I've waited to speak to you all these days. It's Tom Jones, sir.

ALLWORTHY Tom Jones?

MRS. WATERS To be hanged tomorrow.

ALLWORTHY I know.

MRS. WATERS You won't remember me. It's long years past.

ALLWORTHY Yes?

MRS. WATERS I was Jenny Jones, your sister's maid.

ALLWORTHY Tom's mother.

MRS. WATERS I was never his mother. It's time you knew of it, sir. His true mother could never bear to admit her shame. He was your sister's son.

ALLWORTHY Bridget's son?

MRS. WATERS You were away that time, for months before he was

born. Mistress Bridget asked that I should take the
shame on me.

ALLWORTHY You lost your name so lightly?

MRS. WATERS What's shame to a servant? Cross two parishes and
she's new-made a virgin. This is your own flesh and
blood, Mr. Allworthy, that you can leave to be hanged.

ALLWORTHY If he were my son, he still killed a man.

MRS. WATERS To save himself. I saw those witnesses bribed.

ALLWORTHY Saw them?

MRS. WATERS By a pale face in a black coat. I know neither name
nor motive and I've seen nothing of him since. Search
high or low, he's not been in London these past weeks.

ALLWORTHY Captain Fitzpatrick drew on Tom?

MRS. WATERS Knocked him down and drew on him.

ALLWORTHY You saw it?

MRS. WATERS I saw him down and the other with his sword out.

ALLWORTHY And they were bribed to perjury?

MRS. WATERS Yes. I saw that done.

ALLWORTHY Then we must find the man and the witnesses.

MRS. WATERS There's little time.

ALLWORTHY My nephew will help. He's always stood Tom's friend,
even against me. (*He calls offstage* L.) Mr. Western! Mr.
Blifil! Step in here, if you please. If we could but find
the man who gave the bribes, and bring him face to
face with the witnesses—

MRS. WATERS As well look for a black drop in a rainstorm.

ALLWORTHY He must have had some motive for malice—
(BLIFIL *comes in, followed by* MR. WESTERN D.L.)

MRS. WATERS (*interrupting him as she catches sight of* BLIFIL) Him!
It's him, him. Mr. Allworthy, him. There!

ALLWORTHY Mr. Blifil, ma'am?

MRS. WATERS Him it is. He bribed the witnesses.

BLIFIL Who is this poor afflicted woman?

MRS. WATERS And your good, loving, honourable, generous brother
to hang for your money.

ALLWORTHY You're mistaken, ma'am. My nephew has always
pleaded his brother's cause. He has grown up an
honourable, religious man.

WESTERN Aye, and to wed my Sophy.

MRS. WATERS   Not while Tom Jones is alive. Penniless he may be, since you cast him off, but never a woman Tom kissed could set her eyes on him.

WESTERN   That'll be over tomorrow night.

MRS. WATERS   Aye, and you forever safe with your uncle's money. And thinking that once Tom's dead, for very weariness of heart Miss Sophia may marry you. It is him, Mr. Allworthy, there's motive for malice enough and I saw him. I'd never forget a face as sour and cold as that.

ALLWORTHY   There's something here we must look into. Can you help us find the witnesses?

MRS. WATERS   I may be able to.

ALLWORTHY   Mr. Western, be so good as to come with us. And you, nephew.

BLIFIL   Uncle, I have long proved my obedience to you, but I cannot lend myself to this outrage against my person and my integrity.

ALLWORTHY   I see a reason, nephew, which might have bred a hidden hatred in your soul. Come then.

MRS. WATERS   If there is time—
(*They go out D.L. The* D.L. *lighting fades and the prison lighting comes up to dawn. A bell begins to toll.* TOM *gets up.*)

TOM   My time is come. They come for me.
(*The* CONSTABLE *comes in D.R. carrying a considerable length of rope. He is very cheerful.*)

CONSTABLE   There now, sir. Bright and early. There's a beautiful shave they gave you. And it's a lovely morning for a hanging. You'll excuse me if I just bind your arms a little, sir. Usual practice, you know, can't break tradition. I'll have those chains off your wrists, and if you would be so good as not to use your liberty in any way violently, there being six strong men outside, as I left there thinking they might come across you all distasteful. There now, sir. (*He has removed the chains from* TOM's *wrists, and hands them, with the stool and the basket, into the wings.*) Now, if you wouldn't mind, sir, just letting the arms hang, sir, if you'll pardon the expression, quite close to the sides, so. Thank you, sir.

(He walks round TOM, *winding the rope round and round* TOM's *arms, tying them tightly to his sides. Then he removes* TOM's *leg irons. and hands them into the wings.)* Oh, I must say I like a gentry hanging. I do, sir. I always look forward to a gentry hanging. They go off with such an air. I get all sorts, of course, but I can always be proud of my gentlemen. Whether it's the stern repentance or the brave devil-may-care, off they go, into the sunrise. Cleanshaven. Noble. There's satisfaction in it for us. Rewarding. Of course, that's private education for you. You don't get that from the grammar schools. And then I like hanging, sir. I never was one for the beheading in the old days. And just lately we've had a nasty crop of treasons with the Pretender. Not but what most of them were Scotch, and that's not the same as hanging human beings, but still. It's untidy, treason. I never could hold with the mess, letting a man watch while you burn his insides, and then dismembering. No, I like a nice, tidy hanging with a tidy corpse your young lady could recognise, only for having a black face and a bit swollen. Red letter day for me, sir, really. Oh and thank you for the most handsome gesture made last night. Very kindly. All of us, sir, of course you'll understand it isn't our custom to drink a gentleman's health. But you may be sure you will be well remembered tonight, when we drink your salvation instead. There, sir. Comfortable?

TOM As can be expected.

CONSTABLE There. What did I tell you? One thing you always get with a gentleman. A quip. Would you be ready, sir?

TOM Yes. *(The light grows stronger. The truck pivots back. Two men bring a ladder and fix it to the R. of the scaffold. A drum beats slowly and a bell tolls.)*

CONSTABLE And don't you worry, sir. One of the best practitioners in the country, you've got. Never drunk on the job. Unconscious in two minutes, dead in ten. Never a failure. Right then, sir.

*(*TOM *and the* CONSTABLE *turn to face upstage. The* PRIEST *and the* EXECUTIONER *come in U.R. followed by*

a crowd of spectators. The PRIEST *is preparing himself
with a discreet drink from a flask. When* TOM *reaches
him he climbs the ladder on to the scaffold. The*
EXECUTIONER *stands at the foot of the ladder and the*
CONSTABLE *indicates to* TOM *that he should be tipped.*
TOM *cannot get at his trousers pocket, so the* CONSTABLE
reaches in, finds some coins and puts them in TOM'S
hand. TOM *holds his hand out as far as he can. The*
EXECUTIONER *takes the money and touches his forelock.*
TOM *climbs the ladder and kneels before the* PRIEST
while the EXECUTIONER *prepares the noose, which hangs
from the gallows crosspiece. The crowd hushes itself
almost to silence while* TOM *prays, and then as he stands
bursts forth with more noise.* TOM *moves under the
noose. The* EXECUTIONER *blindfolds him and begins to
put the noose round his neck. Shouts are heard offstage,
mingled and unintelligible.)*

ALLWORTHY   Make way, make way, quick, let us pass!

MRS. WATERS   Stop, stop, save him, quick, a reprieve!

WESTERN   Get, gurt lummock, get, tally ho, and away, tally ho!
(SOPHIA *appears, with* HONOUR *and* ALLWORTHY'S MAN-
SERVANT *D.L. The shouts come closer and the com-
motion grows.)*

ALLWORTHY   Out of our way! In the King's name! Let us pass!

MRS. WATERS   Tom, Tom! Let us through! A reprieve, a reprieve!

WESTERN   What ho, Somerset! Out, out, tally ho, gone away!
(*A drum-roll rises to a crescendo.* ALLWORTHY, MRS.
WATERS *and* WESTERN *burst through the crowd and
come D.C.* ALLWORTHY *has a legal document in his hand
which he waves above his head.)*

ALLWORTHY   Stop! Stop! A reprieve!
(ALLWORTHY *goes up to the scaffold and hands the document up to the* EXECUTIONER, *who glances at it and
then gives it to the* PRIEST. *There is a moment of sus-
pense while the* PRIEST *reads it. Then he nods to the*
EXECUTIONER, *who makes a signal offstage to cut off the
drum and bell. The crowd cheers and goes on cheering
until* TOM *confronts* ALLWORTHY, *when it falls silent.
The* EXECUTIONER *takes the noose and blindfold off* TOM

and unties his arms. TOM *leaps down from the scaffold into the arms of two of the crowd and then comes downstage.* WESTERN *is R. of him,* ALLWORTHY *L., and* SOPHIA *L. of* ALLWORTHY. TOM *sees* ALLWORTHY, *hesitates and then takes his hand and falls on his knees before him. Then he gets up and sees* SOPHIA.)

TOM Sophia! (*He goes to her and, taking both her hands, falls on his knees before her. The crowd is now still and silent.*)'

WESTERN Sophy girl, I stick by what I said. 'Tis bread and water if tha'll none marry Allworthy's only heir.

(TOM *looks back at him.*)

Sha't have her, sha't have her. Now your true birth and Blifil's treachery are known, she's thine, boy, and thy uncle's money!

SOPHIA In all this time, I have at last learned to be an obedient daughter.

TOM Sophy girl! (*He flings his arms around her. Then, holding her hand, he turns to the audience.*)

So at the last my dear Sophia is won
And all my cares and restlessness are done.
(*He crosses to stand C., between* ALLWORTHY *and* WESTERN.)
With my dear uncle kindly at my side,
With Squire Western when the huntsmen ride,
In Somerset, at home, where I belong,
(*He comes downstage.*)
If Molly's married, how can I go wrong?
Forgive me, ladies, that I loved your sex,
And let no adamantine frown perplex
The beauty I have seen when you have smiled.
And gentlemen, whom beauty has beguiled,
Stand yet by virtue. Turn away from sin.
At best, you may a dear Sophia win.
At worst, if fortune brings no such caress,
Yet stand by virtue: it will tire you less.

CURTAIN

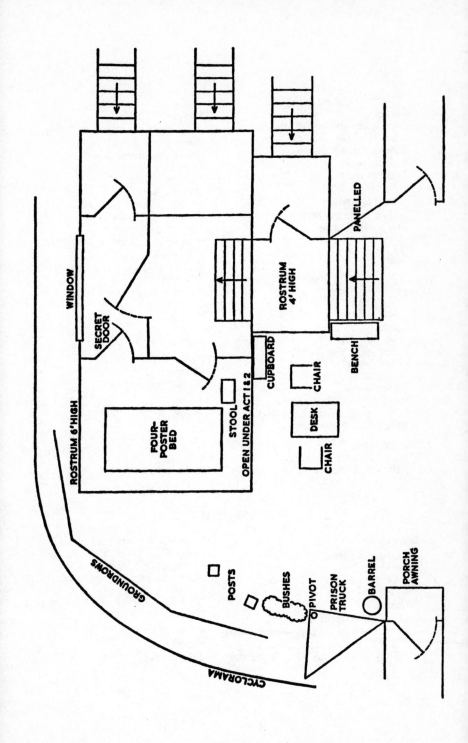

PROPERTY LIST

ACT I

Bedroom
Four-poster bed, fitted drapes,
mattress and bedding
Swaddled baby on bed
Bedside table
Tray on table
On it:
Two pill boxes
Four medicine bottles
One upright chair

Study
Desk
In desk drawer:
Bank draft
On desk:
Ink well
Sand box
Leather folder
One quill pen
One letter
One letter
Two books
High-backed carver chair R. of desk
Small upright chair L. of desk
Bench beside staircase

Molly's house
Porch at door R.
Rain barrel U.S. of porch

Offstage
Two single candlesticks (electric)
Birdcage with trick linnet
Small country chair
Inventory
Twelve knives
Twelve forks
Twelve dessert spoons
Sixteen teaspoons
Large pewter tray
Two-branch silver candelabra
(electric)
Pewter tankard
Doctor's box
Court record book

PERSONAL :

DOCTOR
Pocket watch and chain

THWACKUM
Cane
Rustic walking stick

WESTERN
Rustic walking stick

TOM
Ring

MOLLY
Bone hair pins

ACT II

Bedroom
Change dressings on bed
Chair
Table

Parlour
Three-seater settle by stairs
Two small side tables—one each
end of settle
Wheel-backed chair D.C. facing fire

Practical fire-logs burning
Four single candlesticks on table R.
end settle (electric)
Two candlesticks on mantelpiece
(electric)
Wooden bucket with scrubbing
brush and cloth

Offstage L.
Pewter tray

Decanter of cordial
Two goblets
Pewter tankard
Dress for MRS. WATERS' change

Offstage R.

Three bundles clothing
Five cases
Two jewel cases (SOPHIA and MRS.
    FITZPATRICK)

PERSONAL:

CAPT. FITZPATRICK
    Sword in scabbard

TOM
MRS. WATERS
CAPT. FITZPATRICK   } Coins
WESTERN
SOPHIA
MRS. FITZPATRICK

SOPHIA
    Wallet
    Ring

SQUIRE WESTERN
    Riding crop

ACT III

Bedroom

Change dressings on bed
Small dressing table
Small chair
Two-branch silver candelabra on
    dressing table
Book on dressing table

Drawing room

Chaise longue C.
Occasional table U.L. of chaise
    longue
Book on table
High-backed carver chair by stair-
    case
Small side table by chair

Prison cell

Three-legged stool

Offstage L.

Small silver salver
Letters
Three-branch candelabra (electric)

Offstage R.

Document of reprieve
Leather bottle
Pannier basket
Small cloth-covered basket

PERSONAL :

CAPT. FITZPATRICK
    Sword in scabbard
    Leather bottle

TOM
    Sophia's wallet
    Ring
    Sword in scabbard
       (suitable for duel)
    Two letters

ALLWORTHY   } Silver-topped sticks
FELLAMAR

WESTERN
    Rustic walking stick

CONSTABLE
    Set of leg irons
    Set of manacles
    Truncheon
    Bunch of keys
    Length of thin cord
    Nosegay

PRIEST
    Prayer book
    Small bottle